# Gennaro Contaldo

PASSIONE

## The Italian Cookbook

### with photographs by Jason Lowe

headline

Photographs © Jason Lowe
(except all black-and-white photos which are author's own)

First published in 2003 by
HEADLINE BOOK PUBLISHING

10 9 8 7 6 5 4 3 2 1

Cataloguing in Publication Data is available from the British Library.

ISBN 0 7553 1118 3

Photographs by Jason Lowe
Art Direction and Design by Vanessa Courtier
Colour reproduction by Spectrum Colour, Ipswich
Printed and bound in Italy by Canale & C.s.p.A.

Headline Book Publishing, A division of Hodder Headline, 338 Euston Road, London NW1 3BH
www.headline.co.uk   www.hodderheadline.com

302448

# contents

# introduzione

## introduction

I enjoyed the sort of unrestricted, free-range childhood that few children today can even dream of. The mountains were my back garden. The warm, turquoise sea was a perfect paddling pool just yards away from the house where I was born. The tiny village of Minori on the beautiful Amalfi coast of southern Italy was my heaven.

School didn't feature much in my life. I played truant constantly, and my days were spent outdoors, fishing with the local fishermen, hunting with my father, gathering herbs from the mountains for my mother and exploring the countryside. It was the perfect apprenticeship for a chef, and I was already becoming passionate about food.

As soon as I could talk, my large family and our community of neighbours taught me to love and understand the food we ate. Cooking and eating were pleasures entwined in every thread of local life. Good food was central to every family and community occasion.

The excitement I felt as a child, discovering the possibilities of taste and texture and the sheer pleasure of mealtimes, has never faded. I hope this book will bring you some of the joy of my childhood and teenage years. Many of the recipes and techniques I learned all those years ago are still my favourites, and you will find them here.

My father, Francesco, was the first to inspire me. He was a linen dealer by trade but was also a great cook. Unusually for an Italian man, he took on the role of main cook in the family. He had a gift for combining flavours and could create an amazing dish from practically nothing. From my father, I learned the importance of using the best and freshest ingredients. He knew which farms had the finest produce and where to catch the best fish, and he taught me to hunt for game.

On Sundays he was in his element. It was a feast day for every family, and he made ours extra special. When the church bell struck midday, all the children knew it was time to run home. I would immediately drop whatever I was doing and hurry back through the village to my grandfather's house. What a way to work up an appetite! Glorious cooking smells wafted from every house on the way, and I could detect what each family was going to be eating that day. By the time I reached home, my mouth would be watering.

There were always at least 25 people around my grandfather's big table – aunts, uncles and cousins, as well as my four sisters, our parents and me. The dogs and cats waited under the table for us to throw scraps, which flew more generously as the wine flowed freely. The huge kitchen would be filled with the wonderful aroma of smoke from the wood-burning oven. My father was always at the centre, holding court and, more often than not, arguing with my granddad about the

*A proud and emotional day – seeing my father for the first time in several years*

right combination of ingredients – a matter they both took very seriously.

My father was also pretty serious about wanting me to attend school. It wasn't enough that I shared his passion for food; he wanted me to have an education, too. But I angered him by repeatedly playing truant. There seemed to be so many better things to do than go to school. I liked to go down to the sea armed with a hook and spend the day fishing and swimming. On cooler days, I would set off for the mountains to wander through the forests and talk to the farmers.

My mother, Eufemia, didn't mind my playing truant. In fact, she positively encouraged it. She knew she couldn't make me go to school, so she put my time to good use. She sent me to

collect salt from the rocks by the sea, and herbs and mushrooms from the mountains. And she loved it when I went down to the sea and brought home fish.

As an ex-dancer, she was a natural performer, and quite a character. Many village people believed she was a white witch. They turned to her for advice with their problems and swore by her herbal remedies. Fortune-telling was another of her talents. She was respected but people were also rather afraid of her powers.

I adored her. Vivacious and exuberant, always great fun to be with, she was a wonderful mother, and I think she understood me very well. She let me have my freedom but all the while she was teaching me about wild herbs and plants as I gathered them for her remedies. We were very close, and I feel proud that people often say I am like her.

When I was eleven, my father decided on a radical solution to my obvious lack of interest in school. One morning, without any warning, he dropped me off at his friend's new restaurant to work in the kitchen. I worked from seven in the morning until eleven at night all through the summer. Looking back, it was child slavery. It might have been intended to send me scuttling back to the classroom but I loved it. Fascinated by every detail, I was prepared to do anything. Although the chef was strict with me, he taught me a great deal about food. Much to my family's irritation, I began to think I was an authority and started criticising the way they cooked at home.

Living in a small fishing village, you can't help but be aware of nature and the seasons changing around you. You can watch the weather transform in the distance over the sea. You can smell the changes in the earth and sea with each new season. I love the different seasons. The sense of anticipation as you wait for the cherries to ripen on the trees, for instance. You think you can remember

*Mamma, Aunt Alfonsina, my younger sister Adriana and me on the balcony at home*

the taste but when you actually eat them after an eight-month wait, the flavour is sensational. Today it feels as if there are no seasons. You can buy any food you want at any time of year. But it all tastes the same. I can't believe it when I go into a supermarket at Christmas and find cherries there. Real cherries are ready in April, May and June. To me, there is no such thing as a cherry at Christmas.

September has always been my favourite month. The smell of autumn is fantastic. With the first drop of rain, the scent of the dry earth, leaves and herbs comes alive. The wind is fresher and the sea is rougher and colder. In Minori, all the tourists would disappear and the village became mine once again. I would watch the swallows, which had been with us all summer, forming groups high in the sky, ready to emigrate for the winter. The bats and lizards gradually disappeared and the fishermen brought home a different sort of catch.

Officially, it was time for me to go back to school. My teacher paid personal visits to encourage it, but to no avail. I stopped going down to the sea every day but I started going up to the mountains. The game season was beginning. The fruit was ripe on the trees, wild berries were appearing on the bushes and there was an abundance of mushrooms. Autumn is the time for finding and preserving food to enjoy in the cold winter months.

The mountain farmers were curious to know why I was always wandering around on my own. But they were hospitable and kind. I wanted to watch how they lived, what they cooked and ate, and how they preserved food. I was learning all the time.

The village priests knew all about food, too. They used to eat with all the families in their flock but some households – noticeably the ones with good wine to offer – were visited more frequently than others. They would often move on to enjoy pudding with a different family, this time choosing one renowned for its baking.

I was a favourite of Padre Mateo, a very tall priest who looked after the church. He loved children, and used to tell us stories and give us sweets and leftover communion bread. In return, we would do the work around the church for him. He always called on me to carry the cross at the benediction when someone in the village had died. It was a privilege, but I hated the job. I didn't like being in a room with a dead person. It was only made bearable because the grieving families tipped us generously and offered us lots of good food.

*Papá with my younger sister Adriana on the cellar steps*

I came to England in 1969 at the age of 20. It sounded so beautiful. Every young man I knew wanted to go there. England was cool – it had the Beatles – and I had always been fascinated by damp weather. Perfect. The reality, though, was not the glamorous life I had dreamed of. I found myself working as a kitchen porter at Putney General Hospital. It was the only way I could get a work permit. I was appalled by the terrible meals produced there. The kitchen had beautiful equipment and many varieties of fresh meat and vegetables were delivered. But once the food had been cooked, the result was disgusting. They cooked a dish they called 'Italian'. I had never heard of it and I certainly couldn't eat it. The pasta was cooked days in advance and then reheated. Vegetables were boiled to within an inch of their lives.

Eventually, the chef grew tired of my constant complaints and told me I could do breakfast – 400 boiled eggs and toast. With my poor grasp of English, I set out and, instead of boiling, I poached 400 eggs. No mean feat. I was exhausted, but I think the chef was impressed. After that, I was always allowed to help and, if there was a party on, the hospital would ask me to cook.

By day I was a porter at the hospital but by night I worked as a chef in Prego, an Italian restaurant in Soho. It was one of the best Italian restaurants of its day. The head chef was Antonio Ruocco, a very talented chef from the same part of Italy as me. I learned a lot from him before moving on to work in two other London restaurants: a private club for City bankers, under a French chef, and Meridiana in Chelsea, where I was trained by Angelo Cavaliere. When I was just 22, I was appointed head chef at the Talbot Inn, a restaurant in the Midlands. From the Midlands, I moved to Scotland, where I was trained in English cuisine – and also learned the Scottish way to cook. I loved the Highlands, and went hunting and fishing at every opportunity, until I finally decided to return to London. This time I worked in a fashionable spot in St John's Wood for a couple of years. But at that time, Italian food was still considered a bit of a joke in England. The only Italian foods people knew were spaghetti bolognese and ice cream … and that upset me.

I decided to go back to Italy to learn as much as I could about the food of my childhood. I travelled all over Italy for a year, cooking as I went and learning all the time from the finest Italian chefs – famous ones in the big cities and unknown masters in the villages. It cemented my passion for cooking and reinforced my belief in the value of regional and seasonal foods.

I brought my rekindled passion for Italian food back to England and was employed in many Italian restaurants, culminating in Antonio Carluccio's, where I found myself cooking for the great and good, from royalty to football stars.

In 1999, together with my partner, Liz, and my good friend, Gennaro D'Urso, I opened my own restaurant, **passione**, on Charlotte Street in London. We called it **passione** because I have such a passion for creating beautiful food.

Writing this book brought back many memories for me. So it seemed only fitting that we should return to my home town to cook the food that appears in the photographs – and to retrace my childhood footsteps along the beautiful Amalfi coast.

When I breathed the intoxicating, southern Italian air, it was like being born again. I became a child once more. It was wonderful to be able to show off my beloved homeland. We arrived in late summer in the middle of a violent tropical storm – exactly like the night I was born. There was such a deluge at Naples airport that we couldn't get to our car but I was happy to feel the Italian rain on my skin again.

The fortnight we spent there was an emotional roller coaster for me. I saw my father for the first time in years, and wept tears of joy as we embraced. I wanted to thank him for everything he had taught me and given me. Now in his nineties, he had grown very frail since we last met but he was still dressed immaculately in his usual hand-made suit, hand-made shoes and sharp grey Trilby.

Our arrival caused quite a commotion in the village. We stayed in a lovely villa overlooking a bay and as soon as we were through the door, gifts of food began to arrive from every direction. Antonio Rocco, my first boss in England, turned up with great basketfuls of fresh pasta. My old friend, Pepino, brought a goose he had killed specially. Adriana, my sister, turned up with box upon box of typical Italian crockery, pots and pans, and even an antique pasta table. I was thrilled that she brought my mother's treasured glasses for ice cream and her favourite dishes in which to display my food. There was a stream of visitors bringing tomatoes, vegetables, bread and cheeses.

Our villa had a terrace with a wood-fired oven. We cooked everything outside. It was nothing like being in a photographer's studio, or even a restaurant kitchen. This was real cooking and I loved it. I was thrilled that all the recipes worked perfectly, even though we cooked in the rain, in the sun, through thunderstorms and into the night. It was so exciting. The passions of my childhood were still there, unchanged. I loved the fact that I was able to cook on the open fire – in exactly the same way that my mother had cooked. It was almost as if my hands were being guided by an unseen force. I felt my mother's presence so strongly that she might have been standing beside me, watching.

# ingredienti essenziali
## essential ingredients

### Anchovies
Preserved in either oil or salt, anchovies are a must in my store cupboard. I use them in many of my recipes – a couple of fillets gently 'dissolved' in olive oil before adding the other ingredients enhances the flavour without giving an unpleasant fishy taste. Salted anchovies need washing under cold running water. The ones in olive oil need no preparation and I find them perfectly adequate to use in cooking.

### Chillies
I always keep a few fresh red chillies in the fridge, as well as a bunch of dried chillies hanging up in the kitchen. When I run out of fresh chillies I rely on the dried supply. Dried chillies are more concentrated, which means they taste hotter, so use them with caution.

### Dried pasta
I keep at least one type of short dried pasta, such as penne, fusilli or farfalle, one type of long pasta, such as spaghetti or tagliatelle, and a small pasta shape for soups. This means I can prepare different dishes to suit a particular shape.

### Dried porcini mushrooms
You can find dried porcini almost everywhere these days. I generally keep a packet in the cupboard to enhance my mushroom dishes, especially out of season, when I crave that 'wild forest fungi' taste. Before use, soak the mushrooms in warm water for 30 minutes and then drain.

### Essential vegetables
I like to have an onion, some celery, a few carrots and some leeks in store. They form the basis of so many sauces and other dishes that they are known in Italy as *i sapori* – the flavours. They should be finely chopped and sweated gently in a little olive oil at the start of cooking a dish.

### Flour
I use Italian '00' flour for pasta, '0' flour for bread and '00' flour or ordinary plain flour for cakes and pastries. Italian '00' flour is a soft, refined flour and is more expensive than most other flours you will find in supermarkets but it gives much better results. '0' flour is rougher, and full of gluten, which makes it ideal for bread.

### Garlic
I couldn't live without my beloved garlic! Look for garlic bulbs with a pinkish-purple tinge to them, as this means they are very fresh. When garlic is this fresh, the smell is strong but the flavour less intense. When it is dry, it tastes more pungent.

When cooking, I like to crush garlic cloves roughly but leave them whole, sweat them gently in oil to infuse it, then remove them. I also like to slice the cloves very finely lengthways so they add just a subtle flavour to a dish. Always be careful not to burn garlic, or it will taste bitter.

Store garlic in an airtight container at room temperature.

### Herbs
Almost all my recipes include some fresh herbs to enhance the flavour. These days supermarkets sell all sorts of herbs in cellophane packets but I suggest you buy them in pots and keep them on your kitchen windowsill, or grow them in your garden. My favourite herbs are flat-leaf parsley, basil, rosemary, thyme, bay, mint and sage, and I always have at least one pot of each. Besides tasting delicious, they look great in any kitchen and are easy to grow. Oregano is the only herb I keep dried in my store cupboard. Instead of chives, I often use the green part of spring onions.

### Mozzarella cheese
For cooking, mozzarella cheese made from cow's milk (*fior di latte*) is fine, but be sure to buy an Italian make, packed in water. If you find *mozzarella di bufala* (mozzarella made from buffalo milk), then eat it fresh, simply served with a drizzle of good-quality extra virgin olive oil and some salt and black pepper. This is how they eat it in Campania, the home of this wonderful cheese. Or make a traditional *insalata di caprese*: roughly slice the mozzarella and arrange it on a plate with some sliced ripe tomatoes, then drizzle with extra virgin olive oil and sprinkle with salt and fresh basil leaves. Made with good ingredients, this is the king of salads and encapsulates the taste of summer and Italy.

### Oils
Apart from Piedmont and Lombardy in the North, everywhere in Italy produces olive oil, so there is a wide variety available. In order for the oil to qualify as extra virgin, the production process has to meet several strict criteria – for example, the olives have to be hand picked to avoid bruising and then taken to the mill immediately for pressing. Extra virgin olive oil is obtained from the first cold pressing of the olives.

I cannot stress the importance of investing in good-quality extra virgin olive oil. There are so many on the market these days that I suggest you spend a little time investigating which ones you prefer. My favourite is from Liguria. It is not too pungent, but light, delicate and easily digestible. I use it to dress salads, drizzle over grilled fish, meat and vegetables, and basically for all dishes in which the oil is to be eaten raw or hardly cooked.

The process for ordinary olive oil is less complicated, and although there are strict controls they are much fewer then for extra virgin. More abundant quantities are produced and hence it is more economical to buy. I tend to use olive oil from Liguria, Tuscany and Sicily, and always keep a large 5-litre bottle at home. Ordinary olive oil is used for nearly all cooking purposes, as well as for marinades, deep-frying and preserving food.

## Olives
Look for whole, firm olives and always buy unpitted ones. It may take a little time to remove the stones but they taste much better as they have been tampered with less. My favourite are Taggiasca olives – small, brownish ones from Liguria. I never buy flavoured olives, preferring to flavour them myself with perhaps some garlic, chilli and oregano, or some small pieces of lemon and orange.

## Parmesan cheese
This is a cow's milk cheese from Emilia Romagna. I always keep a good hunk of Parmigiano Reggiano (the name for authentic Parmesan cheese) stored in the fridge wrapped in foil or clingfilm and then grate it as necessary for cooking purposes. Parmesan is also delicious to nibble as a snack when you are feeling peckish, or can be served as part of a cheese selection (see page 00).

## Pepper
Black pepper always tastes best freshly ground, so buy whole black peppercorns to use in a pepper mill.

## Salt
I keep three varieties of salt in stock: fine sea salt for seasoning dishes, coarse sea salt for preserving food, and Maldon salt for topping focaccia.

## Stock
When I don't have time to make my own stock, I use powder, of which I keep at least one vegetable and one meat variety in store. I find the powdered variety is more flexible, as you can use as much or as little as you need. It also dissolves much quicker in the boiling water. I particularly like the Swiss Marigold brand.

## Tinned plum tomatoes
Buy tinned whole plum tomatoes and chop them yourself. They tend to have more flavour than the ready-chopped variety.

## Vinegars
I use white and red wine vinegar as well as cider and balsamic vinegar. I usually make my own red wine vinegar from leftover bottles of wine. I pour all the leftovers into a large glass container, place a couple of bits of dried pasta in it, which speeds up the process, and leave it opened for about 20 days, shaking it gently each day. After this time, it should turn into vinegar – if not, leave it for longer. I then transfer the vinegar into smaller glass containers or bottles with corks and use it like any other wine vinegar. I find my home-made vinegar much stronger than the bought variety and delicious on salads.

Balsamic vinegar is produced in Modena, in the Emilia Romagna region. Made from the must of local Trebbiano and Lambrusco grapes, it is cooked at high temperatures until it turns brown and syrupy, then transferred to wooden barrels and left to mature for anything from five to 50 years. This is known as *aceto balsamico tradizionale* and commands very high prices; the older it is, the more expensive it will be. You can buy a cheaper variety of inferior quality, which is matured for only a year and is known as *aceto balsamico di Modena*. This type will do for marinades, when you need a large amount. I suggest investing a little money and going for a five-year-old (or older, if you can afford it) *tradizionale*, to use sparingly in salad dressings, drizzled over boiled meats and poultry, and even over fresh strawberries. You will find that your bottle of balsamic vinegar lasts quite a while, as it is so strong that you need only a few drops at a time.

## Yeast
I prefer to use fresh yeast as much as possible. It can usually be found in good bakeries and some health-food shops. Stored in the fridge, it will keep for up to two weeks. Dried yeast usually has a long sell-by date, so it's always handy to keep some in the cupboard in case you can't get the fresh variety.

# zuppe
soup

**W**e make very fine soup in Italy. I remember having soup as a child and being able to pinpoint every single ingredient used. It tasted nothing like the bland liquid you find in a can these days.

Every member of my family had a favourite soup. My uncle, the baker, who shared my passion for chestnuts, invented a chestnut soup. It was made from sun-dried chestnuts simmered in water with a single clove of garlic, olive oil, rosemary and lemon. Amazingly simple, yet so tasty.

My sister, Phelomena, ate soup because she believed it would help her keep her figure. She was fervent in her soup making, and was rewarded with a remarkable balance of flavours that I haven't tasted since. She made the most beautiful vegetable soup.

My mother loved soup because it was a good way of using up leftovers: cheese that was too hard to grate, scraps of meat and vegetables, even pasta. Despite this, her soups always tasted magnificent. My father liked to make game soup, using up all his hunting bounty.

We had soup all year round, including cold tomato soup in the hottest summer months. Over-ripe tomatoes were passed through a gadget to remove their skins, then oil, basil, lemon and cold vegetable stock were added to the pulp. The taste was amazing.

*Mamma, Aunt Alfonsina, my younger sister Adriana and me on the balcony at home*

# brodo di pollo

chicken broth

Ask your butcher for a boiling chicken, if he has one. If not, use a roasting chicken. The flavour of home-made chicken broth is wonderful, and it is very simple to make: just put everything in a pan and forget about it for an hour and a half. To make it into a soup, either add some pasta for a typical light Italian *brodino* or, for a more substantial soup, add shredded chicken, chopped vegetables and pasta (see opposite).

You can use the broth as stock in other soups, risotto etc. The chicken can be eaten hot or cold as a main course, together with the vegetables, livened up with a little Salsa Verde (see page 83). The chicken is also delicious served cold, drizzled with a little extra virgin olive oil and balsamic vinegar.

**serves 6–8**

1.75 kg (4 lb) chicken

4 carrots, cut in half lengthways
  and then in half again

3 onions, peeled but left whole

6 celery stalks, including lots of
  leaves, squashed and roughly
  chopped

6 cherry tomatoes, squashed

a bunch of parsley stalks, roughly
  chopped

4 litres (7 pints) water

salt

Place all the ingredients in a large saucepan and bring just to the boil. Reduce the heat, cover with a lid and simmer very gently for 1½ hours.

Remove the chicken and vegetables from the pan and strain the liquid through a fine sieve to give a clear broth. Alternatively, if you prefer, you can leave the little bits of vegetables and herbs floating in the broth. The broth will keep in the fridge for 5 days.

To make an Italian *brodino*, place some of the liquid in a smaller saucepan and bring to the boil, then add small dried pasta or small meat-filled agnolotti (see page 30). Reduce the heat slightly and simmer until the pasta is *al dente*. Serve immediately in individual soup bowls with some freshly grated Parmesan.

# zuppa di piselli e menta fresca

pea and fresh mint soup

As soon as spring arrived, we loved to make dishes with the season's new produce, such as fresh peas and herbs. Although the days were hotter, the evenings were still cool, so to keep warm but still have that fresh spring flavour, we would often make a soup such as this one. Try to use fresh peas. It might be hard work to shell such a large quantity but it is well worth it in the end. If necessary, though, you can use frozen peas, or a combination of both.

**serves 4–6**

**a knob of butter**

**2 shallots, finely sliced**

**50 g (2 oz) pancetta, finely diced**

**½ celery stalk, finely chopped**

**500 g (1 lb 2 oz) fresh peas (shelled weight)**

**1 small iceberg lettuce, roughly chopped**

**1 large potato, peeled and cut into cubes**

**1 litre (1¾ pints) vegetable stock**

**15 fresh mint leaves, finely chopped, plus a few sprigs of mint to serve**

**extra virgin olive oil for drizzling**

**salt and freshly ground black pepper**

**for the crostini:**

**a knob of butter**

**small triangles of bread**

Heat the butter in a saucepan, add the shallots, pancetta and celery and sweat gently for a few minutes. Add the peas and stir well, then add the lettuce, potato and stock. Stir well and season with salt and pepper (be careful with the salt, as pancetta is salty and your stock might be too). Cover with a lid, reduce the heat and simmer gently for 15 minutes or until the peas are tender.

Remove from the heat and leave to cool slightly. Then pour into a blender or food processor and whiz until smooth (in batches if necessary). Return the soup to the pan, add the chopped mint and heat through. Check the seasoning and adjust if necessary.

Meanwhile, make the crostini. Melt the butter in a frying pan, add the bread triangles and fry until golden brown on each side.

Serve the soup drizzled with a little extra virgin olive oil, garnished with a sprig of mint and accompanied by the crostini, 2 on the side of each soup plate.

# zuppa di verdure invernali

mixed root vegetable soup

The combination of root vegetables here makes a very tasty soup, simple and economical to prepare and a soothing winter warmer. Because of its cooler climate, root vegetables are more common in the north of Italy – especially scorzonera. This is a strange-looking vegetable, long and thin with a black skin, which needs to be washed well and peeled. The interior is white and has a very pleasant, nutty flavour. If you can't find scorzonera, replace it with salsify or with extra quantities of any of the other root vegetables used. Parsnip is not an Italian vegetable but I have included it in this recipe because it is so easily available in the UK and I love the taste.

serves 6–8

6 tablespoons olive oil

2 garlic cloves, squashed (optional)

1 small onion, roughly chopped

1 leek, roughly chopped

2 celery stalks, roughly chopped

3 scorzonera, peeled and roughly chopped

1 large parsnip, roughly chopped

1 small celeriac, roughly chopped

1 large potato, roughly chopped

1 large carrot, roughly chopped

2 litres (3½ pints) vegetable stock

salt and freshly ground black pepper

croûtons and/or chopped fresh chives, to serve (optional)

Heat the olive oil in a large saucepan, add the garlic, if using, and sweat for 1 minute. Add the onion, leek and celery and stir well. Sweat for a few minutes, then add all the root vegetables and cook, stirring well, for a couple of minutes. Add the stock and bring to the boil, then reduce the heat, cover and simmer gently for 30 minutes, until all the vegetables are tender.

Remove from the heat, cool slightly and then purée in a blender or food processor until smooth (do this in batches if necessary). Return to the saucepan, heat through and adjust the seasoning. Serve immediately, garnished with some croûtons and/or chopped chives, if desired.

Nearly all our soups contained a base of pulses, such as chickpeas or beans. You could buy these very cheaply from the local grocer's. I remember sacks full of dried beans lined up against the wall of the shop. But these weren't good enough for my mother. She didn't trust their quality because she didn't know where they came from. Instead, we bought fresh beans from local farmers in the summer and dried them in the sun. They were so delicious, I always thought they tasted as if the sun had kissed them. My mother used to store them in jars ready for winter use. I really looked forward to autumn and winter, just so I could open the jars and taste the beans again.

Everyone used pulses. In the alleyways of my village, you would invariably see people who looked as if they were panning for gold. In fact, they were sifting through dried beans to pick out any stones that had got mixed up with them in the drying process. You always knew they were going to have soup the next day.

When we wanted to use the dried beans, my mother would soak them overnight. The next day, she added fresh vegetables and maybe some dried meat and cooked them slowly in plenty of water. The taste was out of this world. Bean soup is still one of my favourites.

*Serving up* Zuppa di Borlotti *(see page 23) to Liz and Fortunata, a friend*

passione

# zuppa di borlotti

fresh borlotti bean soup

If you can find fresh borlotti beans at the market or your greengrocer's in spring, buy them; they taste delicious. The pod is the same shape as a broad bean but the colour is a pretty cream and mottled reddish purple.

If you can't get fresh borlotti, soak the dried variety overnight, then drain them and follow the recipe below. You will need to double the cooking time.

**serves 4–6**

120 ml (4 fl oz) olive oil

1 onion, finely chopped

1 carrot, finely chopped

1 celery stalk, finely chopped

¼ leek, finely chopped

400 g (14 oz) fresh borlotti beans (shelled weight)

a handful of parsley stalks, finely chopped

3 ripe cherry tomatoes, quartered

1 garlic clove, crushed

1.5 litres (2½ pints) vegetable stock

a handful of celery leaves

salt and freshly ground black pepper

crostini (see page 18) and extra virgin olive oil, to serve (optional)

Heat the olive oil in a large saucepan, add the onion, carrot, celery and leek and sweat until softened. Stir in the borlotti beans and parsley stalks, then add the tomatoes, garlic and stock and bring to the boil. Reduce the heat, cover the pan and simmer for 50 minutes, until the beans are tender. Stir in the celery leaves, then taste and adjust the seasoning. Serve with crostini and a drizzle of extra virgin olive oil, if desired.

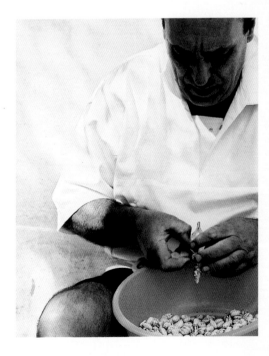

# zuppa di lenticchie

## lentil soup

When I was growing up, we had a wonderful array of pulses to choose from and lentils were a family favourite. We would often make this soup during autumn and winter – it was a tasty way of keeping warm as well as being a good source of protein. Served with some good bread, it is extremely filling and satisfying.

Lentils were sold from huge sacks and the shopkeeper would scoop out the amount you required. Later, at home, we had to sift through them as there were many small stones and impurities. I still sift through my lentils today (old habits die hard), although there is no need, as all shop-bought pulses are now carefully controlled.

If you keep this soup in the fridge for a day or two it will thicken. Either serve it as a stew or thin it down with a little stock.

**serves 4**

4 tablespoons extra virgin olive
   oil, plus a little extra to serve
1 small red onion, finely chopped
1 carrot, finely chopped
1 celery stalk, finely chopped
¼ leek, finely chopped
4 cherry tomatoes, quartered and
   squashed
1 garlic clove, crushed
200 g (7 oz) green or brown
   lentils
1 litre (1¾ pints) vegetable stock
a few celery leaves, finely
   chopped
salt and freshly ground black
   pepper

Heat the olive oil in a large saucepan and sweat the onion until softened. Then stir in the carrot, celery and leek and cook, stirring, for 1 minute. Add the tomatoes and garlic, followed by the lentils. Pour in the stock and bring to the boil. Reduce the heat, cover and simmer gently for 35 minutes, until the lentils are tender. Taste and adjust the seasoning if necessary. Serve garnished with the celery leaves and a drizzle of extra virgin olive oil.

PASSIONE

# stracciatella al pomodoro

## tomato soup with whisked egg whites

Stracciatella is usually a vegetable or chicken broth with a couple of eggs beaten in just before serving to make it more nourishing. In this recipe I have combined a simple tomato soup with whisked egg whites. Make sure you use good ripe tomatoes. To give it colour and body, I have also included some tomato passata. If you prefer not to use the egg whites, you can omit them and you will still have a delicious tomato soup.

**serves 4–6**

600 g (1 lb 5 oz) ripe tomatoes

250 g (9 oz) tomato passata

6 tablespoons extra virgin olive
  oil

750 ml (1 ¼ pints) vegetable
  stock

a handful of fresh basil, plus a
  few leaves to garnish

2 garlic cloves, finely chopped
  (optional)

4 egg whites

1 tablespoon fresh breadcrumbs

4 tablespoons freshly grated
  Parmesan cheese

salt and freshly ground black
  pepper

Skin the tomatoes (see page 163), then cut them into quarters and remove the seeds. Strain the seeds and pulp through a fine sieve over a saucepan to extract as much juice as possible. Add the tomato quarters to the juice in the saucepan, together with the tomato passata, olive oil, stock, basil and garlic, if using. Season with pepper and bring to the boil, then reduce the heat and simmer for 10 minutes. Remove from the heat, allow to cool slightly and then whiz in a blender or food processor until smooth (do this in batches if necessary). Return the soup to the pan, adjust the seasoning and keep warm.

Whisk the egg whites until stiff, then fold in the breadcrumbs and Parmesan. Fold this mixture into the tomato soup and heat through for about 5 minutes, stirring all the time. Serve immediately, garnished with a few basil leaves.

**pasta** pasta

**P**asta is an essential part of all Italian families' diets and mine was no exception. My mother made fresh eggless pasta at least once a week, usually on a Sunday. The process was a magical and exact performance from beginning to end. First, I would be sent up to the mountains to collect the jars of spring water needed for making the best pasta. I would get into such trouble if I used one of the jars to bring down the newts or frogs I caught up there. Spring water creates the most wonderful tasty, shiny pasta with exactly the right firm texture.

The area around us was so mountainous that it was useless for growing wheat, so my father would bring back great sacks of the best wheat from his travels around the region. Much to my mother's frustration, he would insist on grinding it himself. The first press was done with a pestle and mortar, then the rough mixture was put between two massive grinding stones, which he turned slowly. When I was good, my father would let me have a go. It was all very primitive but I loved it; I thought it was real man's work. My mother, on the other hand, hated it. It would drive her crazy. Bits would fly off from the machine and make the most terrible mess, and in any case the resulting flour was too coarse to make good pasta. She went along with it, though, for tradition and to keep my father happy. But when he wasn't looking, she would send me off to the village mill with a sack of wheat to have it ground to the perfect texture – neither too

*Mamma in our garden*

fine nor too coarse. It was a small, incredibly noisy place. They would take your sack of wheat and grind it for you for virtually no charge.

Making pasta was second nature to my mother. She knew instinctively how much water to add, how thick the flour and semolina mixture should be and how it should be kneaded. She was the keeper of the secret of pasta in my family. She always made the pasta in the evening. It was a relaxing family time and we would gather around her big pasta-making table and chat while she worked away. She used a rolling pin to roll out the dough and she stuck to three different shapes. The one I most liked watching her make was fusilli. I collected the long, thick canes she needed to shape it (I found these were also good for making kites, although my mother was never too happy when I poached her pasta-making equipment for kite making!). She would roll the dough out into a long sausage shape, then roll this around the stick – it looked such fun to do. She would also make maccheroni and orecchiette using these sticks. On Sundays we had fusilla, which was much wider then fusilli. We ate it with a ragu (see page 171), which would take about two hours to cook.

I love dried pasta as well as fresh, and there are some recipes for which only dried pasta will do. It supplies a good, *al dente* texture that is impossible to achieve with fresh pasta. When buying dried pasta, always choose one from a traditional Italian manufacturer.

# pasta fresca

## basic pasta dough

Making fresh pasta is not as difficult as it may seem. I make it twice a day at the restaurant, in the morning for lunch and in the afternoon for dinner. I am well equipped there with electric pasta machines and large work surfaces, so it is obviously much easier to make large quantities twice a day. At home I still enjoy making pasta and I do it the traditional way, by hand, then use a small Imperia pasta machine to roll it out. I recommend you purchase one of these before making your own pasta, as it will make life much easier. They are not very expensive and are widely available these days – although when I first came to England, I had to bring my own from Italy. The small one is compact enough for the tiniest of kitchens and easy to store when not in use.

**makes about 300 g (11 oz)**

150 g (5 oz) Italian '00' flour

50 g (2 oz) semolina

2 medium eggs

Mix the flour and semolina together on a clean work surface or in a large bowl. Make a well in the centre and break in the eggs. With a fork or with your hands, gradually mix the flour with the eggs, then knead with your hands for about 5 minutes, until you get a smooth dough; it should be pliable but not sticky. Shape the dough into a ball, wrap in clingfilm and leave for about 30 minutes or until you are ready to use.

Divide the pasta dough into 4 portions and put each one through your pasta machine, starting at the highest setting. As the pasta gets thinner, turn down the settings until you get to number 1 and the dough is almost wafer thin.
Place the sheet of pasta on a lightly floured work surface and use according to your recipe.

**Eggless fresh pasta** This is invaluable for vegans or anyone who cannot eat eggs. Simply substitute 120 ml (4 fl oz) hot (not boiling) water for the eggs and make as above.

# agnolotti ripieni di carne macinata

agnolotti filled with meat

In Italy this is traditionally made from leftover roast meat mixed with chopped herbs and grated Parmesan. If you want to make meat ravioli but don't have any leftover roast meat, follow this simple recipe using minced beef and pork. Serve with melted butter and fresh sage leaves, or with a tomato sauce of your choice (see pages 169-71).

**serves 4**

1 quantity of Basic Pasta Dough
 (see page 29)

To make the filling, heat the olive oil in a small pan, add the onion and garlic and cook until softened. Add the meat and cook until well browned all over. Then add the thyme and parsley and season with salt and pepper. Raise the heat, pour in the wine and let it bubble until completely evaporated. Remove from the heat, discard the garlic and allow the mixture to cool a little. Place in a food processor with the Parmesan and whiz for about 30 seconds, until finely chopped. Transfer to a bowl and check the seasoning.

Divide the pasta dough into quarters and use it one piece at a time, keeping the rest wrapped in clingfilm so it doesn't dry out.

*The harbour in Amalfi has never changed*

**for the filling:**
3 tablespoons olive oil
1 small onion, finely chopped
1 garlic clove, crushed but left
    whole
100 g (4 oz) minced beef
100 g (4 oz) minced pork
1 tablespoon fresh thyme leaves
a handful of fresh flat-leaf
    parsley, finely chopped
4 tablespoons white wine
2 tablespoons freshly grated
    Parmesan cheese
salt and freshly ground black
    pepper

Roll the pasta out in a pasta machine, or roll it out with a rolling pin on a lightly floured work surface until it is so thin you can almost see through it. Cut it into rounds with a 3 cm (1¼ inch) cutter and put a small amount of the filling on each one. Fold each circle in half to make a pasty shape and press the edges down with your fingertips to seal. Press the filling down a little with your finger, roll it gently over in half and then fold back the corners (see page 38).

Bring a large saucepan of lightly salted water to the boil, drop in the agnolotti and cook for about 3 minutes, until *al dente*. Drain and serve with a sauce of your choice.

**Alternative meat fillings**  You could use minced raw lamb and follow the above recipe, omitting the thyme or use left-over roast meat with a flavouring, for example, roast lamb and mint, roast duck and chestnuts, or roast beef with thyme. Simply shred the left-over meat and chop very finely in a food processor. Add the appropriate flavouring, plus some grated Parmesan cheese. Bind together with an egg.

# conchiglioni ripieni al forno

baked pasta shells filled with cheese

Baked pasta (*pasta al forno*) is very common throughout Italy and includes the popular lasagne and cannelloni. In southern Italy there is a baked pasta dish made for special occasions that is based mainly on rigatoni, with a variety of other ingredients including meatballs and boiled eggs. It is very rich, as most baked pasta dishes tend to be, but I would like to share my lighter version of *pasta al forno*, which is simply based on cheese and tomato sauce. Here I have filled large pasta shells with cheese and fresh basil. You could also fill them with leftover roast meat (see page 31), as an alternative to agnolotti (this way you don't have to make the pasta dough).

If you don't want the hassle of filling shells, you can make baked pasta with any cooked short dried pasta mixed with tomato sauce and topped with cheese. It is also a good way of using up leftover pasta – again, just mix with a little sauce and cheese and bake.

**serves 4**

16 conchiglioni rigati
  (large pasta shells)

1 quantity of Salsa di Pomodoro
  (see page 169)

3 tablespoons freshly grated
  Parmesan cheese

1 ball of mozzarella cheese,
  sliced

**for the filling:**

150 g (5 oz) ricotta cheese

1 ball of mozzarella cheese, very
  finely diced

2 tablespoons freshly grated
  Parmesan cheese

16 large fresh basil leaves

salt and freshly ground black
  pepper

Preheat the oven to 200°C (400°F, Gas Mark 6). Cook the pasta shells in plenty of lightly salted boiling water until *al dente*. Drain well (make sure you empty the shells of water) and leave to cool.

To make the filling, mash the ricotta with a fork, stir in the diced mozzarella, Parmesan and some salt and pepper to taste and mix well. Shape the mixture into 16 balls, wrap each ball in a basil leaf and place in a cooled pasta shell.

Pour a layer of the tomato sauce over the bottom of an oven-proof dish and place the filled shells on top. Pour over the remaining tomato sauce, sprinkle over the Parmesan and top with slices of mozzarella. Cover with aluminium foil and bake for 35 minutes. Remove the foil and bake uncovered for 5 minutes. Serve immediately.

PASSIONE

An unofficial but considerable pasta trade went on between families in my village. Certain individuals became renowned for their superior pasta-making abilities and their services were always in demand. When my mother was too busy to make her own pasta, rather than go to the shop to buy some I was sent around the village to barter for it. It has to be said that this was a job I enjoyed. One of the families that made great pasta also had a number of very pretty daughters. Needless to say, I was a very willing errand boy to this house.

My family used to turn up their noses at commercially made pasta but I was strangely drawn to the village's pasta factory. I was fascinated by the massive machines and the dusty bags of flour that were scattered around the floor. The pasta made there seemed to taste better than other commercial pasta. I think it was the combination of fresh sea air, sunshine, spring water and the care put into making it. The factory was right on the sea front, with big doors that opened out to overlook the beach. I used to hover in the entrance and watch the teams of men and women at work. Despite the machines, it was still a manual job. The pasta was pushed through the machines by hand and people waited underneath them to catch the pasta as it came out.

After shaping, the pasta was strung across long canes and hung from the ceiling to dry. It was amazing to see so much pasta in one place, all hanging down from the ceiling with people working below. Once it had dried, it was put outside in the sun to harden off. It's unbelievable now to think that the pasta was put on an area outside the factory that was really just part of the pavement, but people accepted it as part of life then.

*Preziosa, the pasta lady*

# ravioli ripieni di ricotta e limone con salsa di burro e menta

ravioli filled with ricotta and lemon, served with butter and mint

This recipe comes from Minori, my home village, and was given to me by Antonio, the local pasta maker. Lemon and pasta may seem a strange combination but it is actually very good, and dishes like spaghetti with lemon and black pepper are quite common. When I tried this recipe in England, I found that I had to keep adding more lemon zest and juice. The lemons in Italy are much more pungent, so less is needed. When you make the filling, taste it and if necessary add more lemon – the zest only, otherwise it might become mushy.

**serves 4**

1 quantity of Basic Pasta Dough
  (see page 29)

**for the filling:**
225 g (8 oz) ricotta cheese
4 tablespoons finely grated lemon
  zest, plus a little extra to garnish
2 teaspoons lemon juice
2 tablespoons freshly grated
  Parmesan cheese
salt

To make the filling, place the ricotta in a bowl and crush it with a fork, then mix in the lemon zest and juice, Parmesan cheese and some salt to taste. With the help of 2 tablespoons, form the mixture into balls about 2 cm (3/4 inch) in diameter and set aside.

Divide the pasta dough into quarters and use it one piece at a time, keeping the rest wrapped in clingfilm so it doesn't dry out. Roll the pasta out in a pasta machine, or roll it out with a rolling pin on a lightly floured work surface into a paper-thin rectangle. Lay the pasta sheet on the work surface with a short edge nearest to you. Put balls of the filling in a line down the pasta

*With Antonio the pasta maker from Minori*

**for the sauce:**

100 g (4 oz) butter

30 fresh mint leaves, plus a few
    sprigs to garnish

4 teaspoons lemon juice

4 tablespoons freshly grated
    Parmesan cheese

sheet about three-quarters of the way in from one side, spacing them about 2.5 cm (1 inch) apart. Fold the sheet lengthways in half and press with your fingertips between the balls of filling to seal. Cut round the filling with a ravioli wheel or a sharp knife. Gather up all the trimmings, re-roll and repeat. It's important to work quite quickly, so the pasta doesn't dry out. When you have finished, repeat with the remaining pieces of dough.

Bring a large saucepan of lightly salted water to the boil, drop in the ravioli and cook for about 3 minutes, until *al dente*. Meanwhile, make the sauce. Put the butter in a large frying pan with the mint leaves. Add the lemon juice and cook on a gentle heat until the butter begins to bubble.

Quickly drain the pasta, reserving a couple of tablespoons of the cooking water. Add the pasta to the frying pan, together with the reserved cooking water to help give the sauce a little more moisture. Mix in the Parmesan cheese and serve immediately, garnishing each portion with some grated lemon zest and a sprig of mint.

**Alternative potato, cheese and mint filling**  This filling is traditionally used in a Sardinian speciality known as *culurzones*. They are quite a complicated shape but the filling is delicious, and perfect for simple ravioli. As a sauce to accompany this pasta, I would choose either Pomodori in Bottiglie (see page 170) or simply melted butter and sage topped with freshly grated Parmesan cheese. Mix 2 large boiled and mashed potatoes with 1 egg, 50g (2 oz) each of povolone, pecorino and Parmesan cheeses and a handful of finely chopped fresh mint leaves. Use to fill ravioli, following the instructions above.

*Overleaf: left page (clockwise from top) tortellini, cappelletti, agnolotti, cappelletti, ravioli, coppole, gnocchetti and fusilli (centre); right page (clockwise from top) tagliolini and tagliolini nero di seppia, conchiglie, orecchiette, spirali, scialatelli and paccheri (centre)*

40

PASSIONE

# spaghetti con fave, pomodorini e caprino

spaghetti with broad beans, cherry tomatoes and goat's cheese

This is a light, spring/summer dish that is extremely simple to prepare and looks lovely and colourful. Without meaning to, it has the colours of the Italian flag – green, red and white. For maximum flavour, do use fresh broad beans if possible. I use the soft Italian caprino cheese, which you can find in good Italian delis. Alternatively, you can use any soft, mild Welsh or French goat's cheese. Avoid strong goat's cheeses, as they will overpower the delicate flavours of the other ingredients.

**serves 4**

300 g (11 oz) fresh broad beans
(shelled weight)

300 g (11 oz) cherry tomatoes,
quartered and deseeded

120 ml (4 fl oz) extra virgin olive
oil, plus a little extra to serve

2 garlic cloves, finely chopped

20 fresh basil leaves, plus a few
extra to garnish

300 g (11 oz) spaghetti

100 g (4 oz) mild goat's cheese,
diced

salt and freshly ground black
pepper

Blanch the broad beans in a large pan of lightly salted boiling water for 1 minute, then drain, rinse in cold water and drain again. Remove the skins. Put the tomatoes, olive oil, garlic, basil and some salt and pepper in a large bowl and mix well. Then stir in the broad beans and leave to marinate while you cook the pasta.

Cook the spaghetti in a large pan of lightly salted boiling water until *al dente*. Drain and add to the tomato and broad bean mixture, together with the goat's cheese. Mix well and serve immediately, sprinkling some freshly ground black pepper, a drizzle of olive oil and a few basil leaves on top of each portion.

# linguine al granchio

## linguine with crab

I used to fish for crabs quite a lot as a child but the crabs found on my shore were very small, so to get a meal out of them you had to catch plenty and spend many hours cleaning them. It was not until I came to England that I discovered the large, meaty crabs on the shores of Cromer in Norfolk. I believe England's crabs are excellent quality and what better way to enjoy them than with pasta?

**serves 4**

2 medium-sized live crabs

300 g (11 oz) linguine

**for the base sauce:**

6 tablespoons olive oil

1 large onion, finely chopped

1 small leek, finely chopped

2 carrots, finely chopped

2 garlic cloves, squashed and finely chopped

a handful of parsley stalks, finely chopped

150 ml (¼ pint) white wine

12 cherry tomatoes, squashed

500 ml (17 fl oz) vegetable stock

**to finish the sauce:**

4 tablespoons olive oil

2 garlic cloves, finely sliced lengthways

1 red chilli, finely chopped

the leaves from the parsley stalks (above)

120 ml (4 fl oz) white wine

salt and freshly ground black pepper

Either ask the fishmonger to kill the crabs for you, or do it yourself (see page 96) but make sure you reserve the pieces of shell.

To make the base sauce, heat the olive oil in a large pan, add the onion, leek, carrots, garlic and parsley stalks and cook gently until soft. Stir in the crab shells and sauté for a minute. Then add the wine and tomatoes and cook for a couple of minutes longer. Pour in the juices from the crab and the stock, bring to the boil and simmer for 10 minutes. Remove from the heat, take out all the crab shells and place them in a bowl. Pour a little hot water over the shells, as if washing them, and then add the water only to the sauce. Place the sauce back on the heat, bring to the boil and simmer for 3 minutes. Strain through a fine sieve into a bowl, pressing down on the vegetables with a wooden spoon to obtain as much liquid from them as possible. Discard the vegetables and crab shells.

Bring a large saucepan of lightly salted water to the boil and cook the linguine in it. Meanwhile, to finish the sauce, heat the olive oil in a large frying pan, add the garlic and chilli and sweat until softened. Add the parsley leaves and crab meat and season with salt and pepper. Pour in the wine and evaporate, then add the base sauce and simmer for 2 minutes. Taste and adjust the seasoning. Drain the linguine about a minute before it is done and add to the sauce. Continue to cook for a minute in the sauce, then serve.

# penne con funghi, gamberi e zafferano

penne with mushrooms, prawns and saffron

Mushrooms and prawns may seem an unusual combination but they are quite delicious together and remind me of my hunting days in the autumn. I would pick mushrooms, go fishing and
take it all home where my father would make a similar pasta dish to this one. The base sauce
can be prepared a day or two in advance and kept in the fridge. Don't be alarmed about using
the prawn heads and shells – this is what gives the sauce so much flavour.

**serves 4**

200 g (7 oz) fresh raw tiger
   prawns or other large prawns

300 g (11 oz) penne

**for the base sauce:**

120 ml (4 fl oz) olive oil

1 onion, roughly chopped

1 leek, roughly chopped

2 small carrots, roughly chopped

8 cherry tomatoes, halved and
   slightly squashed

120 ml (4 fl oz) white wine

120 ml (4 fl oz) water

**to finish the sauce:**

120 ml (4 fl oz) extra virgin olive
   oil

2 garlic cloves, finely chopped

½ red chilli, finely chopped

100 g (4 oz) button mushrooms,
   finely sliced

a handful of fresh flat-leaf parsley,
   roughly chopped

120 ml (4 fl oz) white wine

a pinch of saffron

salt and freshly ground black pepper

Twist off the heads from the prawns and peel off the shells.
Roughly chop the heads and shells and set aside. Slice the
prawns lengthways into strips and set aside.

To make the base sauce, heat the olive oil in a pan, add the
onion, leek, carrots and tomatoes and sweat for a couple of
minutes. Add the prawn heads and shells and season with salt
and pepper. Pour in the wine, simmer for 1 minute, then add the
water. Cover the pan and simmer gently for 4–5 minutes, until
the vegetables are tender, then remove from the heat and leave
to cool. Whiz to a fairly smooth consistency in a food processor,
then strain into a bowl through a fine sieve, pressing the mixture
with a spatula to extract as much juice as possible. You should
get about 140 ml (4½ fl oz) of fairly thick sauce.

Bring a large saucepan of lightly salted water to the boil and cook
the penne until *al dente*. Meanwhile, to finish the sauce, heat the
extra virgin olive oil in a large pan, add the garlic and chilli and
sweat until softened. Add the mushrooms and parsley and stir-fry
for a minute. Then add the strips of prawn, season and stir-fry for
another minute. Add the wine and simmer until it has reduced by
half, then add the base sauce and simmer for a couple of minutes.
Drain the pasta and add to the sauce, still on the heat. Stir well
and cook for about 30 seconds. Remove from the heat, stir in
the saffron and serve immediately.

One of the greatest adventures I ever had was while I was trying to catch a tuna fish. I was 15 years old and had gone out with two friends for a day's fishing. We set out to sea in a tiny boat with a box of sardines. It was a lazy, sunny day and we were all just taking it easy when, out of the blue, the thick, brown line we had hanging off the side of the boat started to pull. I took hold of it and realised the enormity of the situation. Whatever was on the other end of the line was huge. The three of us tried to pull it in, but it started dragging the boat down. It was terrifying but exciting. We fought with the fish for about three hours, until it was too exhausted to fight any more.

Together, we tried to pull the 95-kilo tuna on to the boat but it was just too big. So we finished it off and dragged it in behind the boat on a hook. I felt sad for this amazing old fish but very proud of myself. I had always wanted to catch a really big fish.

Some fishermen on a motorboat had stopped and made fun of us when we were struggling with the tuna, but I think they were just jealous of our gigantic catch. By the time we got back to shore, word had spread that we had caught an enormous fish and a big crowd had gathered on the beach to witness our return. We were heroes. My mother and father were at the front of the crowd. I jumped on to the beach, my head held high, and my mother stepped forward and gave me a clout round the head, then launched into a public tirade about how stupid I had been. She had been worried sick about me and my father just thought it was funny. Still, it was the biggest fish I'd ever caught and it made me a hero in the village.

PASSIONE

# tagliatelle con tonno, limone e rucola

tagliatelle with tuna, lemon and rocket

This needs hardly any cooking and tastes delicious! When I was growing up in Italy, we didn't have tinned tuna but in late spring/early summer my mother would buy fresh tuna from local fishermen and preserve it in oil, so we could have it all year round. Tinned tuna in extra virgin olive oil has the best flavour; don't buy it in brine or spring water.

**serves 4**

300 g (11 oz) tagliatelle

4 tablespoons extra virgin olive oil, plus extra for drizzling

1 garlic clove, finely chopped

2 x 160 g tins of tuna in extra virgin olive oil, drained

a handful of rocket, plus a little extra to serve

grated zest and juice of 1 lemon

salt and freshly ground black pepper

Cook the pasta in a large pan of boiling salted water until *al dente*. Meanwhile, heat the olive oil in a large pan, add the garlic and sweat for 1 minute. Lightly mash the tuna with a fork and add to the pan, then add the rocket. Season with salt and pepper and stir in the lemon zest and juice.

Drain the pasta and add to the sauce. Mix well together and serve immediately, drizzled with a little extra virgin olive oil and with a little extra rocket on top.

*Watching Preziosa, the local pasta lady, at work in the hills of Minori*

# tagliolini al tartufo nero

tagliolini with black truffle

A truffle is a fungus, found underneath the ground, which can be detected only by specially trained dogs. There are three types of truffle in Italy: the very expensive white truffle from the Alba region in Piedmont *(Tuber magnatum)*, the black winter truffle from Umbria *(Tuber melanosporum)*, and the black summer truffle *(Tuber aestivum)*, again mainly from Umbria. They are quite ugly to look at and resemble small potatoes, with a hard, black skin. For a special occasion, do splash out on a small fresh truffle and try this recipe.

I dedicate this recipe to my eldest son Michael, who appreciated the subtle but sophisticated taste of this fungus from an early age.

**serves 4**

400 g (14 oz) fresh or dried
   tagliolini (or tagliatelle)
500 ml (17 fl oz) vegetable stock
40 g (1½ oz) black truffle,
   shaved on a small mandolin or
   with a very sharp knife
40 g (1½ oz) butter
2 teaspoons truffle oil

Cook the pasta in a large saucepan of lightly salted boiling water until almost *al dente*. Meanwhile, put the stock in a large frying pan with a few shavings of truffle and bring to a gentle simmer, just to infuse the stock with the truffle. Drain the pasta and add to the stock. Raise the heat and continue to cook the pasta for a minute or so until about three-quarters of the stock has evaporated. Stir in the butter and truffle oil and mix in about half the truffle shavings. Remove from the heat and serve immediately, with the remaining truffle shavings on top.

PASSIONE

# pennette con fiori di zucchina

pennette with courgette flowers

I find courgette flowers a real treat. When I first came to England, I discovered that the flowers were destroyed here so the courgettes would grow bigger. I was distraught! I remember asking an old neighbour if he wouldn't mind giving me the flowers from his courgette plants. He looked at me suspiciously and I told him they were to decorate the kitchen. I think he would have thought I was mad if he knew I ate them! Fortunately, you can now find courgette flowers during the early summer in some good greengrocer's, or you could grow your own courgettes. Picking the flowers regularly will help the plants to grow.

**serves 4 as a starter**

120 ml (4 fl oz) olive oil

2 garlic cloves, crushed but left
  whole

2 anchovy fillets

2 small onions, finely chopped

2 small courgettes, finely sliced
  lengthways

200 ml (7 fl oz) vegetable stock

20 courgette flowers, torn in half

20 fresh basil leaves

250 g (9 oz) pennette
  (or another type of short pasta)

20 g (¾ oz) Parmesan cheese,
  freshly grated

extra virgin olive oil, for drizzling

salt and freshly ground black
  pepper

Heat the olive oil in a large pan, add the garlic and cook gently until golden. Remove the garlic from the pan and add the anchovy fillets. Stir with a wooden spoon until the anchovies have almost dissolved into the oil, then add the onions and cook gently until softened. Add the courgettes and stock, followed by the courgette flowers and basil. Bring to a gentle simmer and cook, stirring, over a medium heat for a couple of minutes, then season with salt and pepper to taste.

Meanwhile, cook the pasta in a large pan of lightly salted boiling water until *al dente*, then drain. Add the pasta to the sauce, mix well and stir in the Parmesan. Serve immediately, drizzled with some extra virgin olive oil.

PASSIONE

# farfalle con piselli, pancetta e ricotta

farfalle with peas, pancetta and ricotta

This quick and simple pasta dish is very nutritious. I usually like to serve about 75 g (3 oz) pasta per person, but here I have used only 200 g (7 oz) for four people because the sauce is quite filling. You could use other pasta shapes, such as fusilli, spirali or penne.

**serves 4**

200 g (7 oz) farfalle

1 tablespoon olive oil

50 g (2 oz) pancetta, cut into
   thin strips

1 small onion, finely sliced

100 g (4 oz) peas (fresh or
   frozen)

120 ml (4 fl oz) water

120 g (4½ oz) ricotta cheese

salt and freshly ground black
   pepper

freshly grated Parmesan cheese,
   to serve (optional)

Cook the pasta in a large pan of lightly salted boiling water until *al dente*. Meanwhile, make the sauce. Heat the olive oil in a large pan, add the pancetta and cook until translucent. Add the onion and cook for a few minutes, until softened. Stir in the peas and water, season with black pepper and cook for 2–3 minutes, until the peas are tender. Remove from the heat, stir in the ricotta and mix well.

Drain the pasta, reserving 1–2 tablespoons of the cooking water, and add to the sauce with the reserved cooking water. Mix well and allow the moisture to be absorbed slightly. Check the seasoning, then serve immediately with a little Parmesan, if desired.

# trofie con pesto, fagiolini e patate

trofie with pesto, green beans and potatoes

I came across this dish when I was in Liguria a few years ago. Trofie pasta is made with durum wheat flour and water (no eggs are used), then shaped by hand into small spirals that have pointy ends and are thicker in the middle. This type of pasta takes longer to cook than most; check the instructions on the packet but you will find it usually takes 15–20 minutes. The thicker middle bit always remains *al dente*.

Pesto also comes from Liguria, where delicate extra virgin olive oil is produced and lovely sweet basil grows in abundance. You can find ready-made pesto everywhere these days but it really is worth making your own. You could use a food processor but when the sauce is made by hand with a pestle and mortar it is slightly crunchier, and you can taste all the ingredients much more. Fresh pesto keeps in the fridge for about a week.

**serves 4**

250 g (9 oz) trofie

4 small new potatoes, scrubbed
　　and cut into quarters

20 green beans, trimmed and cut
　　in half

freshly grated Parmesan cheese,
　　to serve (optional)

**for the pesto:**

75 g (3 oz) fresh basil

2 tablespoons pine kernels

1 garlic clove

½ teaspoon coarse sea salt

200 ml (7 fl oz) extra virgin olive
　　oil (Ligurian, if you can get it)

2 tablespoons freshly grated
　　Parmesan cheese

First make the pesto. Remove and discard the stalks of the basil; set the leaves aside. Place the pine kernels, garlic and salt in a mortar and grind to a paste with a pestle. Add a few basil leaves and some of the olive oil and grind and stir with the pestle. Continue like this until you have used up all the basil leaves and about half the olive oil and the sauce has a silky consistency. Then add the remaining oil and the Parmesan and mix well together.

Bring a large saucepan of lightly salted water to the boil and add the pasta, potatoes and green beans. Cook until the pasta is *al dente* and the vegetables are tender. Drain and arrange on 4 individual plates, making sure that each portion has equal amounts of pasta and vegetables. Pour a couple of tablespoons of pesto sauce in the centre and sprinkle with some Parmesan, if desired. Serve immediately.

*Making pesto in my genuine Roman mortar*

# insalata di pasta

crunchy pasta salad

Very simple to make and extremely nutritious – pasta is a good source of carbohydrates, while all the raw vegetables are an excellent source of vitamins. If there are any of the vegetables you don't like, just add more of what you do like.

PASSIONE

serves 4

14 green beans, boiled until
 *al dente* and sliced lengthways
 in half
1 small courgette, peeled and
 sliced into very thin strips
1 small celery stalk with leaves,
 finely chopped
½ small green pepper, cut
 lengthways into thin strips
5 baby spring onions, trimmed
 but left whole
a handful of fresh broad beans,
 boiled until *al dente*, then
 skinned and split in half
¼ leek, very finely chopped
8 cherry tomatoes, cut into
 quarters and deseeded
4 asparagus spears, sliced
 lengthways
2 tablespoons finely chopped
 fresh chives
a handful of fresh flat-leaf parsley
 leaves and stalks, finely
 chopped
100 g (4 oz) mozzarella cheese,
 diced
6 tablespoons extra virgin olive oil
juice of ½ lemon
150 g (5 oz) short pasta, such
 as farfalle, penne or fusilli
salt and freshly ground black pepper

Place all the vegetables and herbs in a large bowl with the mozzarella and toss with the olive oil, lemon juice and some salt and pepper.

Cook the pasta in boiling salted water until *al dente*, then drain and rinse in cold water. Add the cooled pasta to the vegetable mixture and mix well together.

*Eating* al fresco *with Manuela and Marco*

**polenta, risotto, gnocchi**

polenta, risotto, gnocchi

As alternatives to pasta, Italians enjoy polenta, risotto and gnocchi. Polenta is usually served as a main course or a side dish. Gnocchi and risotto, however, are served as the primo course, which comes between the antipasto and the main course.

These three dishes are mainly northern in character and were not very common in our household when I was growing up, although we did have our own versions of risotto and gnocchi. Polenta mixed with hot milk was traditionally the staple diet of the poor in the North. This is why we southerners called the people from the North *polentoni* (polenta eaters). When I was young, I thought polenta looked disgusting, and found it hard to believe that northerners ate it daily. I remember my mother occasionally making it for breakfast but more often than not she used it to feed the chickens and pigs. I now know

what a mistake that was, and over time I have come to consider polenta a delicacy. It is delicious accompanied by a heavy meat or mushroom ragu, or simply served with a slice of gorgonzola gently melting over the top.

Cooking traditional polenta well takes a long, long time. Even in restaurants we only cooked it on special occasions, mainly because you have to tend to it for over an hour. The end result is worth it, though. The taste is magnificent after you have added flavour in the form of cheese or vegetables.

*My old friends Gianni, Rino, Alfredo and Guido on the beach in Amalfi*

# polenta concia

## basic polenta with cheese

Polenta is ground maize flour, which is cooked with water for about 40 minutes until it turns into a soft, creamy mass. Once cooked, the polenta is flavoured with lots of butter and cheese and can be served with tomato-based ragu and stews. It can also be left to cool and set, then sliced and grilled to serve as an accompaniment to meat and game dishes. Polenta flour makes an interesting addition to cakes and biscuits instead of ordinary flour and I often use it to sprinkle on baking trays for my bread.

To make the very best polenta, you should use the traditional variety that needs stirring continuously for about 40 minutes. The alternative is quick polenta (*polenta svelta*), which takes only a few minutes to cook. It doesn't have quite the same taste as traditional polenta but it makes a very acceptable substitute if you don't want to stand over the stove for ages.

This recipe is known as *polenta concia*, and is flavoured with butter and cheese. You can omit these if you prefer a lighter version.

**serves 4**

1 litre (1¾ pints) water

salt

200 g (7 oz) polenta

50 g (2 oz) butter

75 g (3 oz) Parmesan cheese, freshly grated

100 g (4 oz) fontina cheese, cut into small cubes

Put the water and some salt in a medium saucepan and bring to the boil. Gradually add the polenta, stirring all the time until it has all been amalgamated. Reduce the heat, as polenta does tend to bubble quite a bit, and beware of any lumps forming. If they do, just beat very energetically until the lumps have dissolved. Stir the polenta with a wooden spoon for about 30–40 minutes, until it starts to come away from the side of the pan. If you are using quick polenta, follow the instructions on the packet. Then add the butter, Parmesan and fontina and mix well. Serve immediately, with Ragu di Pomodoro (see page 171), if desired.

# polenta alla griglia

grilled polenta

Grilled polenta makes a tasty accompaniment to meat and game dishes. It can be made in advance, stored in the fridge for a couple of days and then grilled when necessary. Topped with some preserved vegetables (see page 161), it makes a wonderful antipasto or snack.

**1 quantity of Polenta Concia,
made without the cheese
(see pages 56-7)
a little olive oil**

As soon as the polenta is cooked, pour it into a lightly oiled baking tray. Leave to cool, then cut into slices or use a pastry cutter to cut it into rounds. Place over a hot charcoal grill or on a hot ridged grill pan and cook on both sides until crisp.

You can also fry the polenta. Heat a non-stick frying pan until very hot, then brush with olive oil. Add the polenta and fry on both sides until crisp. The grill, griddle pan or frying pan should be very hot before you add the polenta slices, otherwise they will stick.

*Costantino, Peppe and me enjoying our food!*

# gnocchi di polenta con sugo ai peperoni

polenta gnocchi with a red and yellow pepper sauce

This is a different and more interesting way of using polenta by making the mixture into quenelles and serving them in a sauce, like pasta or gnocchi. You could make the sauce and quenelles the day before, store them in the fridge and when ready just reheat the sauce, add the quenelles and heat through.

**serves 4–6**

500 ml (17 fl oz) water

2 teaspoons salt

25 g (1 oz) butter

120 g (4½ oz) quick-cook
   polenta

25 g (1 oz) fontina cheese, diced

25 g (1 oz) Parmesan cheese,
   freshly grated

**for the sauce:**

3 tablespoons extra virgin olive
   oil

2 anchovy fillets

1 garlic clove, squashed but left
   whole

1 small red chilli, left whole

1 red and 1 yellow pepper,
   roasted, skinned and sliced into
   thin strips (see page 163)

50 ml (2 fl oz) white wine

50 ml (2 fl oz) vegetable stock

First make the sauce. Heat the olive oil in a large pan, add the anchovy fillets and cook, stirring, over a low heat until they have almost dissolved into the oil. Add the garlic and chilli and fry until the garlic becomes golden brown, then remove and discard the garlic and chilli. Add the strips of pepper and sauté for a few minutes. Pour in the wine and let it bubble until it evaporates slightly, then add the stock and simmer for 5 minutes. Remove from the heat and set aside.

To make the polenta gnocchi, put the water in a large saucepan with the salt and butter and bring to the boil, stirring all the time until the butter melts. Reduce the heat and gradually add the polenta, stirring constantly with a wooden spoon. Cook according to the directions on the packet until you obtain a medium-thick consistency. Mix in the cheeses and remove from the heat.

Make quenelles with the polenta mixture by taking a tablespoonful of it, scooping it off the spoon with another tablespoon and then scooping it back again until it is a neat oval shape, turning the spoons against each other. Have a bowl of cold water ready by your side so that the tablespoons can be dipped in the water after each quenelle is made – this makes it easier for the quenelle to slide off the spoon.

Put the pepper sauce back on a moderate heat. Place the quenelles in the pepper sauce and heat through. Serve immediately.

When I was a child, I knew that rice was cultivated in northern Italy but I knew nothing of the special rice fields that were flooded and drained. I thought rice could be grown in back gardens, like the vegetables and grain we ate. I also thought that rice was the same all over the world. How wrong I was. Italy, or more particularly Lombardy, is the capital of risotto rice.

I mastered the art of making good risotto in my years travelling around Italy as a chef, and quickly learned that even within Italy there are different types of

rice. Every Italian chef I have worked with has argued that a specific grain is best for making risotto. In my opinion, no particular one is superior; they all have their own flavour and texture. As long as you use one of these Italian grains, your risotto will taste delicious. Once I tried to use three or four different types to make a risotto. I thought I was being clever but the textures were all different and it tasted terrible.

After I left home, I sometimes went back to visit my family and cooked them risotto. They just couldn't understand why you should have to spend half an hour or more standing by a pot, constantly stirring and adding stock. I think one of the reasons risotto never really took off in southern Italy was that the climate is so warm that it really isn't comfortable to stand at a hot stove for long.

*Aged 17 on the beach in Minori*

# risotto

## basic risotto

The first rule when making risotto is to use the correct Italian rice, such as Arborio, Carnaroli or Vialone Nano, because they can absorb a huge amount of liquid without breaking up. Next, use good stock and the risotto will taste wonderful. Home-made stock is ideal but a good quality cube or powder will suffice. Your stock can be any type, depending on the flavours you are adding. For a basic risotto, use vegetable or chicken stock. Cook the risotto at a gentle simmer and stir constantly to make sure it absorbs the liquid evenly and doesn't stick to the pan. The stock should be added a little at a time, making sure that each batch has been absorbed by the rice before adding more. The stock must be hot, otherwise the risotto will stop cooking when it is added and the dish will be ruined, so keep it simmering in a separate pan. You may find you need a little more or less stock than the amount specified in the recipe, so always have a little extra ready.

If you follow these few simple rules then there is no reason why you shouldn't make successful risotto. Just like pasta, it can be a homely, comforting dish using vegetables, or a chic dinner-party affair with wild mushrooms, seafood or even truffles.

**serves 4**

1.5 litres (2½ pints) vegetable or chicken stock

3 tablespoons olive oil

1 medium onion, finely chopped

375 g (13 oz) Arborio or other Italian risotto rice

50 g (2 oz) butter

50 g (2 oz) Parmesan cheese, freshly grated

salt and freshly ground black pepper

Put the stock in a saucepan and bring to a gentle simmer. Leave over a low heat.

In a medium-sized heavy-based saucepan, heat the olive oil and sweat the onion until soft. Add the rice and stir until each grain is coated with oil. You will notice the rice becoming shiny. At this stage, add a couple of ladlefuls of the hot stock and cook, stirring all the time, until it has been absorbed. Repeat with more stock. Continue adding the stock in this way until the rice is cooked, which usually takes about 20 minutes. To check if it is done, taste the rice; it should be soft on the outside but *al dente* inside.

Remove from the heat and beat in the butter and Parmesan with a wooden spoon so all the ingredients are well combined and creamy. In Italy, this procedure is known as *mantecare*. Taste and adjust the seasoning. Leave to rest for 1 minute then serve.

PASSIONE

# risotto con piselli, fave e zucchini

risotto with fresh peas, broad beans and courgettes

All the flavours of spring in one dish! Obviously, if you can't find fresh produce you could use frozen peas and beans. However, do try it with fresh ones, if possible. They are easily available in spring, and it really does make a difference to the taste – and also the texture, since fresh peas and beans are crunchier. This makes an excellent vegetarian main course.

serves 4

2 courgettes

1.2 litres (2 pints) vegetable stock

4 tablespoons olive oil

½ celery stalk, very finely chopped

½ leek, very finely chopped

350 g (12 oz) Arborio rice or other Italian risotto rice

120 ml (4 fl oz) white wine

100 g (4 oz) fresh peas (shelled weight)

100 g (4 oz) fresh broad beans (shelled weight)

25 g (1 oz) butter

25 g (1 oz) Parmesan cheese, freshly grated

salt and freshly ground black pepper

First of all prepare the courgettes. Trim off the ends, then cut off the skin in thick strips (a good 5 mm [¼ inch] thick) and discard the white flesh, which tends to be mushy (you could save it to add to vegetable stocks). Chop the green part of the courgettes very finely and set aside.

Put the stock in a saucepan and bring to a gentle simmer. Leave over a low heat.

Heat the olive oil in a medium-sized heavy-based saucepan. Add the celery and leek and sweat until softened. Add the rice and stir until each grain is coated with the oil. You will notice the rice becoming shiny. At this stage, add the wine and keep stirring until it evaporates. Then add the peas, beans and courgettes and mix well, making sure that the vegetables do not stick to the pan. Add a couple of ladlefuls of the stock and cook, stirring all the time, until it has been absorbed. Repeat with more stock. Continue adding the stock in this way until the rice is cooked, which usually takes about 20 minutes. To check if it is done, taste the rice; it should be soft on the outside but *al dente* inside.

Remove from the heat and beat in the butter and Parmesan with a wooden spoon. Taste and adjust the seasoning. Leave to rest for 1 minute, then serve.

PASSIONE

# risotto all'accetosella

risotto with sorrel

Sorrel has a lemony flavour and grows wild but you can also buy a cultivated variety. It's an easy plant to grow in your garden. Usually, sorrel is added to enhance sauces that accompany fish, but its citrus tang also works extremely well with Parmesan cheese.

When we opened passione, I put this dish on the very first menu and now, four years later, am unable to take it off. It has become one of the restaurant's signature dishes.

**serves 4**

1.5 litres (2½ pints) good
    vegetable stock
3 tablespoons olive oil
1 small onion, finely chopped
1 celery stalk, finely chopped
375 g (13 oz) Arborio or other
    Italian risotto rice
150 g (5 oz) sorrel
75 g (3 oz) butter
50 g (2 oz) Parmesan cheese,
    freshly grated
salt and freshly ground black
    pepper

Put the stock in a saucepan and bring to a gentle simmer. Leave over a low heat.

Heat the olive oil in a medium-sized heavy-based saucepan. Add the onion and celery and sweat until soft. Add the rice and stir until each grain is coated with oil. You will notice the rice becoming shiny. At this stage, add a couple of ladlefuls of the stock and cook, stirring all the time, until it has been absorbed. Repeat with more stock. Continue adding the stock in this way until the rice is cooked, which usually takes about 20 minutes. To check if it is done, taste the rice; it should be soft on the outside but *al dente* inside.

Remove from the heat, add the sorrel, butter and Parmesan and beat well with a wooden spoon to obtain a creamy consistency. Taste and adjust the seasoning. Leave to rest for 1 minute, then serve.

passione

# risotto 'terrone'

## southern Italian risotto with vegetables

This is the way risotto is made in southern Italy and I remember my mother would often do it like this. It does not include butter and Parmesan and you do not follow the usual risotto method. However, it is much easier to make. The end result is similar but without the creaminess you get with the northern risotto. If you like risotto but don't have the patience to stir it for 20 minutes, then try this alternative.

**serves 4**

1 small onion, sliced

1 small leek, sliced

2 carrots, chopped

1 medium potato, peeled and cut into large chunks

2 Jerusalem artichokes, peeled and cut into small chunks

300 g (11 oz) Arborio or other Italian risotto rice

4 tablespoons extra virgin olive oil, plus extra for drizzling

750 ml (1¼ pints) vegetable stock

salt and freshly ground black pepper

freshly grated pecorino cheese, to serve

Place all the vegetables in a saucepan with the rice, olive oil and stock. Cover with a lid and bring to the boil. Then reduce the heat to very low (the contents should not even be simmering) and cook, covered, for 25 minutes. Do check from time to time to ensure that the rice is not sticking to the pan – if it does, give it a quick stir and add a little more liquid. After 25 minutes, the rice will have absorbed all the liquid and the risotto is ready to serve. Check the seasoning, sprinkle with the pecorino and drizzle with some extra virgin olive oil, if desired.

*Talking to Peppe over a bowl of risotto*

We love gnocchi in the south of Italy. You will find them in restaurants all year round, served plain or with tomato sauce, game or cheese. I could happily eat them every day.

My father knew how to make remarkably fine, soft gnocchi. You could taste the delicate flavour of the potato through the sauce as the gnocchi melted in your mouth. His secret was his rather dubious source of very tasty potatoes. They were grown by his friend high up on the hill under the cemetery wall in Minori. Every time we ate gnocchi my father would mention this. He said they tasted so good because the potatoes he used were full of fertiliser from the dead bodies in the cemetery. I knew it wasn't true but was still disgusted at the thought. My father would just sit there and chuckle but my mother would get upset and say that he was being blasphemous.

When I came to England, there were many varieties of potato and I was confused as to which one to use. I experimented with several until I came across the King Edward and bingo! Perfect!

Gnocchi are usually made with mashed potatoes but can also be made with ricotta, pumpkin or even bread. As they tend to be quite heavy, they are best with simple sauces, such as tomato and basil, butter and sage, or pesto.

*Padre Silvio on the streets of Polvica, Tramonti – a hilltop village above Minori*

# gnocchi di patate ripiene di asparagi con salsa al balsamico

potato gnocchi filled with asparagus with a butter and balsamic sauce

If you like potato gnocchi, these are a real treat. I have used asparagus as my filling, because I find it fresh and light, but you could use a variety of ingredients – peas, broad beans, mixed vegetables, meat, mushrooms. Basically as long as the ingredients are very finely chopped, cooked and mixed with a little grated Parmesan cheese, you have a filling.

The sauce I have chosen is a classic butter and sage one, but I have added a few drops of balsamic vinegar at the end. I find the balsamic cuts the richness of the gnocchi and gives a characteristic tangy flavour.

**serves 6**

250 g (9 oz) floury potatoes, such as King Edward

150 g (5 oz) plain flour

20 g (¾ oz) cornflour

2 eggs

salt

Place the unpeeled potatoes in a pan of lightly salted water, bring to the boil and simmer until tender. Keeping the potatoes whole like this means they don't absorb water; if you prefer, you can bake them in the oven.

**for the filling:**

1 courgette

3 tablespoons extra virgin olive
  oil

1 large spring onion, finely
  chopped

4 large asparagus spears, peeled
  and finely chopped (discard
  about 2.5 cm [1 inch] from the
  bottom, as this is tough)

4 tablespoons water

4 tablespoons freshly grated
Parmesan cheese

salt and freshly ground black
  pepper

**for the sauce:**

50 g (2 oz) butter

a handful of fresh sage leaves

2 tablespoons freshly grated
  Parmesan cheese

a drizzle of balsamic vinegar

While the potatoes are cooking, make the filling. Prepare the courgette (see page 162) and then chop the green part very finely. Heat the olive oil in a small pan, add the spring onion and sweat until softened. Then add the asparagus and courgette and sauté over a medium heat for a minute. Season with salt and pepper, add the water and simmer for a few minutes, until the vegetables are tender but still a little crunchy. Place the filling mixture in a bowl, leave to cool and then stir in the Parmesan.

Once the potatoes are cooked, drain and leave to cool. Peel and discard the skin and mash the potatoes. I prefer to use a potato ricer, or 'Italian masher', which is like a giant garlic press. I find you get a much smoother mash without any lumps.

Place the mashed potato in a large bowl with the flour and corn-flour. Add the eggs and some salt and mix well until you get a smooth but slightly sticky dough. Place on a floured work surface and with a rolling pin roll out to a thin sheet about 3 mm (1/8 inch) thick. Cut into rounds with a 7.5 cm (3 inch) pastry cutter. Place a teaspoon of the filling in the centre of half the rounds. Cover with the remaining rounds and press down the edges with your fingers to seal. Re-roll the trimmings to make more gnocchi.

Bring a large saucepan of lightly salted water to the boil and drop in the gnocchi. At first they will sink; as they come up to the surface, cook for a further 2 minutes (remember these are filled gnocchi and much thicker than normal ones, so they need a little longer to cook through).

Meanwhile, make the sauce. In a large pan, melt the butter over a medium heat, add the sage leaves and mix in the Parmesan cheese. As the gnocchi are done, drain and place in the butter sauce. Mix together well. Drizzle some balsamic vinegar over the top and serve.

# gnocchi di pomodori secchi con salsa alle olive nere

sun-dried tomato gnocchi with black olive sauce

**If you like sun-dried tomatoes, you will love this recipe. You add very finely chopped sun-dried tomatoes to a basic potato gnocchi mixture, work into a dough, then shape and cook in boiling water until they come up to the surface.**

**serves 4**

**500 g (1 lb 2 oz) floury potatoes, such as King Edward**

**120 g (4½ oz) plain flour**

**2 egg yolks**

**12 whole sun-dried tomatoes (not the ones preserved in oil), soaked in lukewarm water until softened**

**salt and freshly ground black pepper**

**for the sauce:**

**4 tablespoons olive oil**

**1 small onion, finely chopped**

**2 garlic cloves, squashed but left whole**

**120 g (4½ oz) black olives, pitted and roughly chopped**

**a few sprigs of fresh thyme**

**120 ml (4 fl oz) red wine**

Place the unpeeled potatoes in a pan of lightly salted water, bring to the boil and simmer until tender. Once the potatoes are cooked, drain and leave to cool. Peel and mash the potatoes, preferably with a potato ricer to give a really smooth mash.

In a large bowl, combine the mashed potatoes with the flour, egg yolks, salt and pepper. Drain the tomatoes, squeezing out the excess liquid with your hands, then chop them very finely, almost to a pulp – if necessary, once chopped, blitz in a blender or food processor. Add the tomatoes to the potato mixture and mix well to obtain a soft dough. Take large pieces of the dough and roll them into sausage shapes, then slice into 2 cm (¾ inch) squares. Roll each one over the back of the tines of a fork to mark it slightly and give a traditional gnocchi shape.

Place a large saucepan of salted water on the heat to boil. Meanwhile, make the sauce. Heat the olive oil in a large frying pan, add the onion and garlic and sweat until the onion is soft. Add the olives, thyme and wine and simmer until the wine has evaporated. Season with salt and pepper.

Drop the gnocchi into the pan of boiling water and simmer until they rise back up to the top. As they come to the surface, lift them out with a slotted spoon, drain well and add to the olive sauce. Mix well and serve immediately.

# gnocchi di zucca gratinati

pumpkin gnocchi baked with butter and sage

This makes a tasty alternative to traditional potato gnocchi, especially in autumn when pumpkins are plentiful. Pumpkin gnocchi are quite common in northern Italy, and the idea was given to me by Mario, my sous-chef, whose aunt and mother often make them during the pumpkin season.

**serves 6**

a knob of butter

400 g (14 oz) pumpkin (peeled weight), cut into small cubes

225 g (8 oz) ricotta cheese

175 g (6 oz) Italian '00' flour

50 g (2 oz) ground almonds

50 g (2 oz) Parmesan cheese, freshly grated

25 g (1 oz) provolone cheese, grated (if you can't get provolone, a mature Cheddar makes an excellent substitute)

2 egg yolks

a pinch of ground cinnamon

salt and freshly ground black pepper

**for the sauce:**

175 g (6 oz) butter

12 fresh sage leaves, plus a few extra to garnish

40 g (1½ oz) Parmesan cheese, freshly grated

a few flaked almonds (optional)

Melt the butter in a saucepan over a medium heat, add the pumpkin and stir well. Reduce the heat, cover and cook until tender, stirring from time to time and adding 2–3 tablespoons of water if necessary to prevent sticking. When soft, remove from the heat and put in a piece of muslin. Squeeze well with your hands to extract excess liquid. Unwrap the pumpkin and whiz through a mouli-légumes, or mash with a fork or potato masher. Leave to cool.

Preheat the oven to 220°C (425°F, Gas Mark 7). Put the cooled pumpkin purée in a large bowl with all the remaining ingredients and mix well to a creamy but firm consistency. If it is too runny, add a little more flour; if it is too stiff, add another egg yolk. Put the mixture in a piping bag. The opening should be wide enough for the mixture to come out in finger-thick lengths.

Bring a large saucepan of water to the boil. Pipe the pumpkin mixture into 4 cm (1½ inch) long sausage shapes and drop into the boiling water. Be careful not to burn your fingers with the steam. When the gnocchi float up to the surface they are ready. Drain with a slotted spoon and place in a greased ovenproof dish.

To make the sauce, gently heat the butter and sage leaves in a small pan until the butter melts. Pour the butter and sage over the gnocchi and sprinkle with the Parmesan, together with the flaked almonds if using. Place in the oven and bake for 12 minutes or until golden brown. Garnish with sage leaves and serve immediately.

# ndundari con salsa fresca di pomodoro e basilico

pasta dumplings served with fresh tomato and basil sauce

This dish comes from my home village and is made each year to celebrate the feast of the patron saint, Santa Trofimena, on 13 July. It is said to be an old Roman recipe, and is made in the same way as potato gnocchi but using ricotta cheese instead of potatoes. This makes the dumplings much lighter. Each family has its own way of making them but the basic ingredients are always ricotta, flour and eggs, while the sauce varies depending on what you like. I enjoy these dumplings with a simple tomato sauce but they are equally good with pesto (see page 50).

**serves 4**

200 g (7 oz) Italian '00' flour

225 g (8 oz) ricotta cheese

3 egg yolks

20 g (¾ oz) Parmesan cheese, freshly grated

a pinch of nutmeg

freshly ground black pepper

**for the Pomodori in Bottiglie sauce:**

2 x 400 g tins of plum tomatoes, drained and chopped in half

12 large fresh basil leaves

6 tablespoons olive oil

3 garlic cloves, thickly sliced

salt and freshly ground black pepper

In a large bowl, mix the flour, ricotta, egg yolks, Parmesan, nutmeg and black pepper together to form a soft, moist dough. Place on a floured work surface and knead for 3–5 minutes, until smooth. With your hands, roll the dough into a large sausage shape and then cut it at right angles into rectangular shapes about 2 cm (¾ inch) long.

Bring a large saucepan of salted water to the boil and add the dumplings. Wait until they rise to the surface again, then simmer for 2 minutes longer. Meanwhile, make the sauce as page 170.

Lift the dumplings out with a slotted spoon and add to the tomato sauce. Mix thoroughly and serve immediately.

# pesce fish and shellfish

Our house was set on a cliff edge, 30 metres above the sea. I was born there on a stormy night to the sound of crashing waves battering the windows. The sea was the first thing I ever heard and I fell in love with it there and then.

I don't remember learning to swim, it was just something I could always do. I used to swim in the sea every day as a child. I liked to pretend I was all alone on a desert island, running along the shore and screeching like Tarzan, or leaping through the waves like a dolphin and swimming around the bottom of the cliffs with the fish. I would have such arguments with the fish, diving under the water and chasing them around the rocks.

The sea used to come alive with fish in the summer months. Octopus, red and grey mullet, sea bass, bream, groupers, scorpion fish – you name it. I went after them on boats, from the rocks, off the beach. I fished at night and during the day. I was encrusted with sea salt. Even now, if I put my tongue against my arm I can taste the salt.

The sea was part of me and I mastered the art of reading it. It told me what the weather was going to be like, the best time to go fishing and where to find the finest fish. The secret nooks and crannies of the rocks were my private hunting ground. I improvised with my equipment: fashioning together a hook and line, making my own harpoons, or gathering up cast-off pieces of net from the fishermen. The route to the prime fishing spots was not easy, as

*Back from a fishing trip with Gianni (on the left)*

the rocks were sharp and dangerous. I learned to scramble across craggy cliff faces and swim through underwater arches to get to my special fishing spots. When I caught some fish, I often built a small fire and cooked them there and then. My favourite was sardines cooked on a stick.

Sometimes I would collect mussels, limpets and sea urchins. The mussels were small but full of the tastiest meat imaginable, and delicious eaten raw with just a squeeze of lemon. The oysters were even better. To get to the best oysters I had to dive down about four or five metres. I learned to take a big breath and pinpoint exactly where they were, then dart through the water like a torpedo and snatch them off the seabed. I ate them straight away, fresh from the sea.

I always took a lemon on my fishing excursions and it served many purposes apart from flavouring the fish I caught. It quenched my thirst when I was far away from fresh water and acted as a disinfectant if I scraped myself on the rocks. To this day, I always carry a lemon with me. My mother used to tell me that every slice of lemon would give you an extra year of life.

The sea was crystal clear in those coves, and you could see hundreds of small, colourful shrimps darting through the shallow water. These couldn't be caught with a simple hook or net. Instead, I had to make a special trap from very fine net and a ring of metal. It was hard work lying on my front and scooping the tiny shrimps out of the water, but it was worth it because they were extraordinarily sweet to eat and people paid good money for them.

PASSIONE

# carpaccio di trota

raw marinated trout

England and the English were romantic visions of my childhood. I used to dream of dressing as an elegant English gentleman – and fishing for trout in my elegant clothes amid the glorious English countryside. I had heard many stories about fly-fishing and, desperate to try it out, I once spent a whole afternoon catching flies and sticking them on to my hook and line. I don't need to tell you that it was a complete failure.

When I moved to England, I was introduced to the secrets of real fly-fishing. I fulfilled my childhood dream and became a master trout fisherman. Winning the prize for the biggest trout in Walthamstow may not sound very romantic but it was one of my proudest moments.

serves 4

2 very fresh trout fillets

juice of 2 lemons

2 fennel bulbs, very finely sliced

baby salad leaves, to serve

for the dressing:

120 ml (4 fl oz) extra virgin olive
   oil

4 tablespoons lemon juice

salt and freshly ground black
   pepper

Put the trout fillets in a dish, pour over the lemon juice and leave to marinate for about 15 minutes.

To make the dressing, put the olive oil, lemon juice and some salt and pepper in a small bowl and beat well until it thickens a little.

Remove the trout fillets from the lemon marinade and place on a board. With a very sharp knife, cut wafer-thin slivers of trout and arrange evenly on a large plate, discarding the skin. Spoon some of the dressing over and leave for a couple of minutes.

Arrange a few baby salad leaves on 4 serving plates, followed by some fennel, and top with the marinated trout. Beat the leftover dressing and drizzle over the top. Serve immediately.

# ippoglosso con capperi e dragoncello

halibut with caper and dill sauce

I discovered halibut when I came to England. I loved its light, delicate flavour immediately and it has become one of my favourite fish. I have included two recipes for it in this book: here it is served with a simple green sauce, which gives it a Mediterranean flavour.

**serves 4**

4 pieces of halibut fillet, weighing about 200 g (7 oz) each

juice of 2 lemons

4 tablespoons olive oil

salt

**for the sauce:**

6 tablespoons capers

1 garlic clove, peeled

4 anchovy fillets

a handful of fresh flat-leaf parsley

a large bunch of fresh dill

2 tablespoons finely grated lemon zest

120 ml (4 fl oz) extra virgin olive oil

Score the halibut skin with a sharp knife, then place the fillets in a bowl and pour over the lemon juice. Leave to marinate for about 15 minutes.

To make the sauce, place the capers on a chopping board and squash them slightly with the flat of a knife blade. Place the garlic, anchovy fillets, parsley and dill on the same board and chop all the ingredients very finely, mixing them together as you do so. When everything is finely chopped, place in a bowl and mix with the lemon zest and extra virgin olive oil. Set aside.

Remove the halibut from the marinade, pat dry on kitchen paper and season with a little salt. Heat the olive oil in a large frying pan and cook the fish skin-side down for 3–4 minutes, covering it with a lid to prevent the oil splashing everywhere. Turn the fish over and cook the other side, covered, for 3 minutes. About a minute before the end of the cooking time, uncover the pan and spread a little of the sauce over the top of the halibut.

Place a tablespoon of the remaining sauce on 4 plates, place the fish on top and serve immediately with boiled new potatoes.

# ippoglosso con burro e limone

halibut with lemon and butter

This is an even simpler way of serving really good, fresh halibut. Serve with boiled new potatoes and green beans.

**serves 4**

4 pieces of halibut fillet, weighing about 200 g (7 oz) each

juice of 2 lemons

100 g (4 oz) butter

salt

Score the halibut skin with a sharp knife, then place the fillets in a bowl and pour over the lemon juice. Leave to marinate for about 15 minutes. Drain, reserving the lemon juice, and dry on kitchen paper.

Melt 75 g (3 oz) of the butter in a large frying pan (keep the heat gentle, as it is easy to burn butter!), add the halibut and cook for about 3–4 minutes on each side. Then increase the heat, pour in the lemon juice from the marinade and allow to bubble and evaporate slightly. Add the remaining butter and you will see the sauce thicken. Serve immediately.

*With fishermen from Praiano*

PASSIONE

# insalata di merluzzo con fagiolini e salsa verde

hake salad with green beans and salsa verde

A wonderfully delicate fish, hake tends to be undervalued in the UK, although I believe it has experienced a revival lately. It is eaten a lot in Italy, especially in the South, and in other Mediterranean countries. If you can't find hake, you could replace it with cod. The combination of delicate fish, crunchy vegetables and tangy salsa verde is really delicious. *Salsa verde* is Italian for 'green sauce', and it is traditionally used to flavour steamed fish or boiled meats and sausages. If you double or triple the quantities, you can store it in the fridge for up to seven days and use it to liven up meals during the week.

**serves 4**

2 turnips, cut in half and sliced

4 large, flat green beans (such as runner beans or mangetout), sliced on the diagonal into 2 cm (¾ inch ) lengths

100 g (4 oz) fine green beans, trimmed

1 fennel bulb, outer layers removed, heart thinly sliced

500 g (1 lb 2 oz) whole hake or 400 g (14 oz) hake fillet

lemon wedges, to serve

**for the salsa verde:**

a bunch of fresh flat-leaf parsley

25 fresh mint leaves

3 anchovy fillets

1 tablespoon capers

1 garlic clove, peeled

3 cocktail gherkins (cornichons)

6 tablespoons extra virgin olive oil

1 tablespoon lemon juice

1 small teaspoon English mustard

Cook the turnips, large beans and fine beans in a large pan of boiling water until tender. Lift out with a slotted spoon and set aside to cool. Blanch the fennel in the same water for 1 minute, then lift out and set aside to cool. Cook the hake in the same water as the vegetables. If you are using a whole piece of hake, this will take 10 minutes; if you are using hake fillet, only 5 minutes. Drain the fish and leave to cool, then remove all the bones and skin. Break the fish into large chunks.

To make the sauce, chop the parsley and mint very finely on a chopping board with a mezzaluna, if you have one. On the same board, chop the anchovy fillets, capers, garlic and gherkins, gradually mixing and chopping all the ingredients together very finely. You could do this in a food processor but I prefer to do it by hand, as you get more texture. Place in a bowl, add the olive oil, lemon juice and mustard and mix well.

Arrange the fish chunks and vegetables on a large serving dish or individual plates and drizzle the salsa verde over them. Serve with lemon wedges.

# orata all'agrodolce

sea bream fillets in a honey and white wine vinegar sauce

Sea bream is one of my favourite fish and I used to catch lots of them in Italy. This dish has become very popular at the restaurant – the sweet and sour combination of the honey and wine vinegar works extremely well with the chicory and delicate sea bream. Just make sure you have three pans – one for the chicory, one for the sauce and one for the fish. Try it for a dinner party; it's bound to impress your guests!

**serves 4**

4 sea bream fillets

6 heads of chicory

120 ml (4 fl oz) olive oil

120 ml (4 fl oz) water

4 tablespoons honey

200 g (7 oz) butter

220 ml (7½ fl oz) white wine
   vinegar

salt and freshly ground black
   pepper

Score the skin of each sea bream fillet 3 or 4 times with a sharp knife. Season the flesh side with salt and pepper, then set aside.

Cut each chicory head in half lengthways, discard the small, hard central piece, then cut the chicory into cubes. Heat half the olive oil in a pan, add the chicory and sauté over a medium heat for 1 minute. Season with salt and pepper, add the water and cook until the liquid evaporates and the chicory has softened but is still a little crunchy. Set aside and keep warm.

Put the honey, butter and vinegar in another pan over a gentle heat. When the butter has melted, gently simmer the sauce for about 10 minutes, until it thickens to a syrupy consistency and turns golden brown.

Meanwhile, heat the remaining olive oil in a large frying pan, add the sea bream fillets, skin-side down, and cook for about 3 minutes, pressing down on them with a wooden spatula so the fish doesn't curl up. Flip them over and cook the flesh side for another 3 minutes.

Arrange the chicory on a large serving dish or 4 individual plates and place the fish on top. Pour the sauce over and serve immediately.

PASSIONE

# branzino con salsa alla rucola

sea bass with rocket

Sea bass is another of my favourite fish and is very popular on the southern shores of my home in Italy – certainly a fish I would often catch. It has a lovely, delicate flavour and deserves a delicate sauce to go with it, such as this one made with rocket. Wild rocket has a much stronger flavour, so I leave it to you whether you prefer to use that or the milder, cultivated variety. If you have some sauce left over, or make extra, add a couple of tablespoons of extra virgin olive oil to it to make rocket pesto and use to flavour pasta as an alternative to the usual basil pesto.

**serves 4**

4 sea bass fillets

2 tablespoons olive oil

25 g (1 oz) butter

4 tablespoons white wine

salt and freshly ground black
    pepper

**for the sauce:**

1 tablespoon extra virgin olive oil

15 g (½ oz) butter

3 anchovy fillets

2 shallots, finely chopped

1 medium courgette, finely
    chopped

300 ml (½ pint) vegetable stock

200 g (7 oz) rocket, roughly
    chopped, plus a few handfuls of
    rocket to serve

First make the sauce. Heat the extra virgin olive oil and butter in a pan, add the anchovy fillets and cook, stirring, over a gentle heat, until they have almost dissolved into the oil. Add the shallots and courgette and cook until the shallots begin to soften, then add the stock, bring to the boil and simmer for 1 minute. Stir in the rocket, season with black pepper and simmer for a couple of minutes. Remove from the heat, allow to cool slightly, then whiz in a blender until smooth. Return to the pan and stir over a high heat with a wooden spoon until nearly all the liquid has evaporated and the sauce becomes creamy. Remove from the heat and set aside.

Season the sea bass with salt and pepper. Heat the olive oil and butter in a large frying pan, add the sea bass, flesh-side down, and cook over a moderate heat for about 3 minutes or until golden brown. Turn over and cook for another 3 minutes. Turn over again and gently peel off the skin. Add the wine, cover with a lid and cook for a few seconds. Uncover the pan, turn the fillets over, cover with a lid again and cook until the wine evaporates.

Meanwhile, reheat the sauce gently if necessary. Arrange some rocket on a plate, top with the sea bass fillets and pour the sauce either over the fish or on the side, as you wish.

# orata in aqua pazza

whole sea bream cooked with cherry tomatoes

This dish is very typical of all southern Italian coastal regions. Freshly caught sea bream, fresh tomatoes, basil, extra virgin olive oil and garlic – it encompasses the taste of the sea and the flavours of the South. It is an extremely simple dish to prepare and, provided you have the freshest ingredients and good-quality extra virgin olive oil, you can't go wrong. Even if you live in the city and make this dish on a grey miserable day, it will give you the feeling of being by the sea in the warm southern sunshine.

serves 4

175 ml (6 fl oz) extra virgin olive oil

2 sea bream, weighing about 500 g (1 lb 2 oz) each, cleaned and scaled

4 garlic cloves, roughly chopped

20 cherry tomatoes, quartered

a handful of fresh basil leaves, roughly torn

400 ml (14 fl oz) water

1 small red chilli, finely chopped

salt

Heat the olive oil in a large, heavy-based frying pan over a fairly high heat. Add the bream, followed by the garlic, tomatoes, basil and some salt. Pour in the water, turn the heat down slightly and cook the fish for 7 minutes on each side. When you flip the fish over, you will know that it is done if the eye has turned white.

Remove the fish from the pan and place on a large serving dish. Raise the heat, cook the sauce for 30 seconds to concentrate the flavours slightly and then pour it over the fish. Serve immediately, with lots of good bread to mop up the delicious sauce.

# involtini di pesce spada con finocchio

rolled swordfish fillet with fennel

The filling in this recipe has quite a strong flavour and I find it goes really well with the meaty texture of swordfish. Blanched fennel and onion give the dish a freshness and crunchiness. It all takes a little time to prepare but it is simple to make and the results are stunning. I would make it for a special dinner. Ask your fishmonger for loin of swordfish, which you can either take home and slice yourself or get him to slice for you.

**serves 4**

500 g (1 lb 2 oz) swordfish loin,
    cut into 8 thin slices
6 tablespoons olive oil
2 fennel bulbs, thinly sliced
2 onions, thinly sliced
extra virgin olive oil and lemon
    juice for drizzling
a little lemon zest
salt and freshly ground black
    pepper

**for the filling:**
100 g (4 oz) fresh breadcrumbs
2 tablespoons extra virgin olive
    oil
20 large capers in brine, drained
4 anchovy fillets in olive oil,
    drained
1 small garlic clove
a handful of fresh flat-leaf
    parsley leaves
a handful of fresh mint leaves
4 teaspoons grated lemon zest
freshly ground black pepper

Place all the ingredients for the filling in a food processor and whiz until mushy. Take handfuls of the mixture and make 8 rough sausage shapes with it, then set aside.

Gently flatten the swordfish slices with a meat mallet or a rolling pin and season with salt and pepper, if desired (bearing in mind that the filling is quite salty). Place a piece of filling on each slice of swordfish; don't worry if the filling comes apart slightly – just keep gently pressing it together with your fingers. Roll the fish up and secure with toothpicks, ensuring the sides are closed.

Heat the olive oil in a large frying pan, add the swordfish rolls, seam-side down, and fry for about 1 minute, until golden brown. Turn over and cook the other side until golden brown.

Meanwhile, blanch the fennel and onion for 30 seconds, drain well and place on a large serving dish. Arrange the cooked swordfish on top and drizzle with some extra virgin olive oil and a little lemon juice. Scatter over some lemon zest and serve immediately.

passione

# polipo in umido

## stewed octopus

I used to love catching octopus when I lived in Italy, and even more so taking it home for my father to cook. It's a shame they are not popular in Britain, as the sea here is full of them, but it seems they are caught and exported. A great pity, because they really are delicious, either stewed and served warm as in this recipe or dressed with olive oil and lemon to make a salad. I think a lot of people expect octopus to be chewy and tough, hence its unpopularity. The secret of tender octopus is to cook it without adding any liquid, as it exudes a lot of its own. (There is an Italian saying, 'You are like an octopus, go cook in your own juice.') The only liquid allowed is some olive oil to prevent it sticking to the pan. Follow this recipe and you will see how tender it can be – it should melt in your mouth.

**serves 4**

4 tablespoons olive oil

3 garlic cloves, sliced

1 teaspoon capers

4 green olives, quartered

4 anchovy fillets

2 octopuses, weighing about
    400 g (14 oz) each, cleaned
    (ask your fishmonger to do
    this)

10 cherry tomatoes, squashed

a handful of fresh flat-leaf
    parsley, coarse stalks removed

salt

Heat the olive oil in a small saucepan (use one in which the octopus will fit tightly) and add the garlic, capers, olives and anchovies. Once the garlic begins to sweat, add the octopuses and a pinch of salt. Stir well, lower the heat, then add the tomatoes and parsley. Cover with a tight-fitting lid and cook on a low heat for 1 hour and 10 minutes, until the octopuses are very tender. During cooking they will shrink and exude quite a bit of liquid. Adjust the seasoning if necessary, then serve.

As with any love affair, I did have a few rough times with the sea. When I was about 13, I put to sea with a friend for an evening jaunt in my dinghy. We were having so much fun that we didn't notice the wind blowing us further and further from the safety of the shore. We tried to get back but the current was too strong. The people on the beach didn't take much notice of us. When we shouted, they thought we were just a pair of mischievous boys messing around. The truth was, we were stuck.

As it grew dark, we began to get really frightened. The sea was still and the lights of the town were visible for a long time, which kept us calm. But too soon, they disappeared. I felt the bile of panic rising in my gullet. We imagined we were miles away, and talked about ending up in Africa and never seeing home again. Our young imaginations ran wild, turning the murmuring wind into the whisper of dead sailors, the booming of the ocean into sinister creatures trying to dash our flimsy vessel. We cried like babies as we bobbed around helplessly all night long.

The next morning a police boat found us. When we caught sight of it we started to scream with joy. It was part of a search party out looking for us. We were both severely reprimanded, then they took us home – it only took an hour to get back to shore, so we hadn't gone far at all. I was banned from going on a boat again for a very long time, and my dinghy was destroyed. To keep our dignity, we made up stories of our adventures for our friends – the giant fish we had seen and the dolphins that had saved us.

*Michele D'Urso – a fisherman from Praiano*

# cozze 'scappate'

## stuffed mussels with tomato sauce

Because I lived by the sea, mussels were part of my life, and as a child I would pick buck-
etfuls of them during the cooler autumn months. When we had the larger mussels, my
father would often make this dish by removing the mussels from their shells, mixing them with
some stale bread, garlic and parsley and then stuffing the shells with this mixture. Using mussels in this way made an unusual, tasty dish and also meant they would go further to
feed a large family.

If you like mussels, try this dish for an informal supper with friends; it's fun to eat, as
you have to remove the raffia tied round each mussel. Don't use the green-lip mussels
from New Zealand, which are already dead and have had half the shell removed. The
large Cromer mussels from Norfolk are very good, if you can get them.

**serves 4**

12 large mussels

4 tablespoons extra virgin olive
   oil

4 anchovy fillets

1 garlic clove, thinly sliced
   lengthways

½ small red chilli, finely
   chopped (optional)

20 capers

3 tablespoons white wine

a handful of fresh flat-leaf
   parsley, finely chopped, plus a
   few sprigs to garnish

100 g (4 oz) stale bread, cut
   into small cubes

Clean the mussels by washing them in plenty of cold water,
scrubbing them well and pulling off the beards. Holding a
mussel in a cloth, carefully make an incision around the open
part of the shell with a sharp knife and open it gently, taking
care not to break the shell. Discard the little black 'tongue' and
'lips' (i. e. the frill round the edge) of the mussel – although
these are edible they taste bitter, so I prefer not to use them for
this recipe. Remove the flesh and any liquid and place in a bowl.
Keep the empty shells for later.

Heat the olive oil in a pan, add the anchovies and stir with a
wooden spoon until they have almost dissolved into the oil.
Add the garlic, chilli, if using, and capers. Once the garlic turns
golden, stir in the mussels, reserving their liquid for later. Heat
the mussels through, then add the wine and simmer gently for
1 minute. Pour in the liquid from the mussels and stir in the
parsley. Remove from the heat and mix in the bread cubes, then
leave to cool. When the mixture has cooled, place it on a chopping board and chop quite finely with a sharp knife. Transfer to a
bowl and mix well until you get a mushy consistency.

4 tablespoons extra virgin olive
  oil

1 small onion, very finely diced

1 teaspoon dried oregano

2 large green olives, pitted and
  sliced

240 g tin of chopped tomatoes

salt and freshly ground black
  pepper

Dry the mussel shells and, with a tablespoon, generously fill one half of each shell with the mussel mixture. Close the shell, removing any excess filling that escapes, and wrap some raffia around the middle of the shell, tying it round a few times until nice and tight, so the shell cannot open (you could use string, but I think raffia looks much nicer). Trim off any excess raffia and put the filled shells to one side.

To make the sauce, heat the olive oil in a large pan, add the onion and, as soon as it begins to fry, add the oregano, olives and tomatoes. Season with salt and pepper and bring gently to bubbling point. Reduce the heat and simmer for 5 minutes. Add the mussels to the sauce, cover the pan and cook gently for 20 minutes, turning the mussels over half way through. Stir from time to time and, if necessary, add some water to prevent the sauce becoming too dry. Put the filled mussel shells on individual plates, pour a little sauce over and garnish with a sprig of fresh parsley. Serve immediately, and remember to provide finger bowls for your guests.

**Baked stuffed mussels**    This is an alternative recipe, in which the mussels are baked and the tomato sauce omitted. Remove the mussels from their shells and prepare the filling as for Cozze 'Scappate' (see page 92). Then fill both sides of each empty shell with the mussel mixture. Keep the shells open and place on a baking tray. Mix together a handful of breadcrumbs, a handful of flat-leaf parsley, finely chopped, and enough extra virgin olive oil just to moisten. Sprinkle this mixture over the open mussels. Place in an oven preheated to 200°C (400°F, Gas Mark 6) and bake for 15 minutes or until golden brown. Top each mussel with an anchovy fillet and a chopped green olive, drizzle over some extra virgin olive oil and serve with a few green salad leaves. This makes an excellent starter for a dinner party.

PASSIONE

Minori was a fishing village. I used to hang around the fishermen when they came back with their catches, learning from them, teasing them and probably driving them crazy.

Every afternoon my friends and I waited on the beach for the fishermen to return from their trips. Quite often they would bring ashore a mighty turtle, which they had untangled from their nets. The poor creature would be half dead and brought back as a novelty. They may have caught it a few days earlier but they would have tied it to the back of the boat and dragged it to shore as a trophy. Sometimes the well-travelled sailors would take the turtles home to eat, and many people used their shells to decorate their houses. I never liked this. I knew instinctively that these beasts needed protecting.

One day I was alone on the beach when one of the fishing boats returned with a turtle in a poor state, but still alive. I asked the fishermen if I could have it and, using all my strength, I dragged the half-dead beast back into the sea and round to a small cove away from the main beach. I stayed with her all afternoon, willing her to recover her strength. At night I found a rope and tied her to a rock in the cove. The next morning, when I rushed down to check on her, I found to my joy that she was full of life and spirit, flapping around to try and free herself. I cut the rope and watched her swim away effortlessly.

After that, the turtles became my mission. Every time a fisherman brought one ashore, I would try to save it, though usually without as much success. To my relief, the fishermen soon began to understand that the turtles were special and stopped bringing them home.

# gamberoni e granchio con aglio e peperoncino

king prawns and crab with garlic and chilli

**Always use fresh seafood for this dish. Prawns and crab make a great combination but if you prefer not to use crab, just substitute extra prawns. If you find it difficult to extract the crab meat from its shell, ask your fishmonger to do it for you.**

serves 4

2 large live crabs (see method)

175 ml (6 fl oz) extra virgin olive
   oil

12 fresh raw king prawns, shell on

8 garlic cloves, sliced lengthways

2 red chillies, sliced lengthways
   into strips

2 handfuls of fresh flat-leaf
   parsley leaves

250 ml (8 fl oz) white wine

1 lemon, cut into quarters,
   to serve

salt

Either ask the fishmonger to kill the crabs for you, without boiling them, and reserving their juices, or kill them yourself (if the fishmonger does it, you will have to use them as soon as you get home). To kill them yourself, wrap each crab in clingfilm or roll it up inside a thick plastic bag, then wrap in newspaper. Place on a chopping board and whack as hard as you can with a rolling pin, which should kill the crab instantly. Unwrap the crab (all the juices will be saved in the clingfilm or plastic bag), twist off the tail flap, break up the claws and remove all the flesh, trying to keep it in chunks. Put all the crab meat in a bowl and set aside.

Heat the olive oil in a large frying pan, add the prawns and cook for 1 minute over a high heat. Turn them over and cook the other side for another minute. Add the garlic, chillies and crab chunks, season with salt, then reduce the heat and cook for a couple of minutes with the lid on. Add the parsley, increase the heat and add the wine and the reserved juices from the crab. Bubble until evaporated, then serve immediately, with lemon quarters and lots of bread to mop up the juices.

PASSIONE

*Antonio D'Urso – Michele's cousin – also a fisherman*

# pesce conservato
## preserved fish

Preserving fish is an old tradition and, although its original purpose was to deal with a large catch, preserved fish is still eaten today as a delicacy rather than out of necessity. Here are some of the most popular preserved fish used in Italian cooking.

### Acciughe

You can buy anchovies preserved in either oil or salt. For both types, fresh anchovies are gutted, layered with sea salt and left for about a month. They are then filleted and packed in jars or rinsed of the salt and placed in jars or tins with olive or vegetable oil. See page 12 for tips on using anchovies in cooking.

### Baccalá

This is cod preserved in salt. It was traditionally known as 'poor food', and was eaten by people who lived inland and did not have access to the sea. Cod was the cheapest fish available and was preserved in large quantities, then kept in the store cupboard. However, it has become quite fashionable these days and commands a high price.

   You can buy baccalá in pieces, which have to be soaked in several changes of fresh water for at least 24 hours before use, thereby removing the salt and softening the flesh. In some areas of Italy, such as Liguria, Venice and Naples, baccalá is very prominent on the menu. It is delicious steamed or boiled, then simply dressed with some extra virgin olive oil and lemon juice, eaten warm or cold as a salad, or cooked in a tomato sauce with black olives. It also makes delicious fish cakes and fritters.

## Bottarga

This is cured roe of grey mullet and tuna, produced and consumed mainly in Sicily and Sardinia. It can be used like mosciame (see below), but is more commonly grated over seafood pasta dishes. You can find it in good Italian delicatessens.

## Mosciame

This air-dried fillet of tuna has become quite a delicacy on many menus. It is available in Italian or Spanish delicatessens. Serve thinly sliced, drizzled with some extra virgin olive oil and lemon juice and accompanied by preserved vegetables (see page 161) as an alternate antipasto to cured meats.

## Pesce affumicato

Smoked fish is becoming increasingly popular in Italy and swordfish, tuna, halibut and sturgeon are just some of the varieties available. Arrange an assortment of thinly sliced smoked fish on a large plate, drizzle with lemon juice and serve with mixed baby salad leaves and rocket for an antipasto or light lunch.

## Stoccafisso

This is air-dried cod. It is sold whole and should be soaked in several changes of fresh water for about 24 hours before use. It also helps to tenderise it if you bash it with a mallet before soaking. Cook it in the same way as baccala (see opposite).

# carne

meat, game,
poultry

The back yard of my childhood home was like a small farmyard. There were chickens scratching about in the dirt, lots of rabbits and guinea pigs, and we always had a pig. Every Sunday, we bought meat from one of the three village butchers. We only ate meat once or twice a week but it was truly fresh and we knew where it came from, whether it was the farm or our own back garden. Markets full of live animals – rabbits, chickens, lambs and cows – were part of our lives. We saw animals as a source of food, yet we cared for them and loved them as if they were our pets.

Every Thursday, a bullock was slaughtered in Minori. It was a fascinating event for the children. Great groups of us used to sit on the slaughterhouse wall to watch the gruesome spectacle. The butcher was a bull of a man himself, with a jutting chin. The killing was so cruel and brutal that to our childish eyes it looked like the crucifixion of Jesus. The butcher would tie the bullock's head to a post and bash it hard with a large mallet. Then he slit its throat and drained off all the blood. Finally the bullock was lifted up with large, heavy chains to be gutted and skinned.

People are so removed from the source of their meat these days. You go into a supermarket and see endless rows of pre-packaged poultry, meat and game. It's difficult to associate meat with live animals. For me, it was part of my culture. We respected animals because we knew they were our food. I never saw my mother buy a chicken or pigeon at the butcher's. She had a pigeon coop and she would take the birds out as she needed them.

*Aged 8 with live pigeon and chicken*

By the time I was 11, my father was wise enough to see where my heart lay. During the summer holidays, he found me a job in a fine restaurant run by one of his friends — a great chef by the name of Alfonso. I adored the job, but I think I must have been rather a handful, if only because of my boundless enthusiasm.

As a very junior waiter, I was permitted to greet customers and tell them what was on the menu, but I was not yet entrusted with the important task of taking orders. However, I invented a special responsibility of my own. Almost immediately, I discovered that I could predict people's orders from their reaction when I recited the menu. I would run straight into the kitchen and prepare the ingredients necessary for those dishes, ready for the chef to cook them. Alfonso thought he was losing his mind when, time after time, he went to the preparation table only to find his work already done. He was afraid he had done it himself and then forgotten about it. Eventually he caught me in the act and, after much shouting and swearing, he banned me from the kitchen for the rest of the day. Later, he calmed down, and when he realised how keen I was to cook, he found me work in the kitchen.

Alfonso's restaurant had chickens, rabbits and sometimes even lambs in the back yard. We killed what we needed each day. If the chef ran out of chicken in the middle of a shift, I'd have to run out and prepare another. It might sound gruesome but it meant that all our meat was very fresh.

My time in the restaurant taught me about every sort of meat and every way to cook it. I learned not to waste anything; we used every last scrap.

# antipasto di pesche e prosciutto crudo di parma

antipasto of fresh peaches and Parma ham

Parma ham with melon, Parma ham with figs … both wonderful combinations, but in the middle of a warm summer why not with peaches? It makes a lovely and refreshing starter, but you must use ripe peaches. If you can find them, the small organic ones are out of this world. I dedicate this recipe to Dominique, who loves Param ham so much she would have it at every meal.

**serves 1**

**1 ripe peach**

**a few slices of Parma ham, very thinly and freshly cut**

**a handful of rocket**

**extra virgin olive oil**

**freshly ground black pepper**

Remove the skin from the peach – this is made easier by immersing the peach in boiling water for a minute. Cut the peach in half and discard the stone. Arrange on a plate with the Parma ham and rocket. Drizzle with some extra virgin olive oil and grind over some black pepper.

# vitello alla genovese

## veal slow-cooked with onions

This is an old recipe from the Campania region, and not from Genoa as the name suggests. In the days of the old Italian maritime republics (Genoa, Amalfi, Venice and Pisa), this dish was made for Genoese sailors when they docked in Amalfi, hence the name. Although it takes three hours to cook, it is an extremely straightforward dish to make and you get two courses from just one pot. The onion sauce is used to flavour pasta as a starter, or primo, and the veal joint is served as a main course. Try it for a different Sunday lunch.

**serves 4–6**

1 kg (2¼ lb) veal joint

3 garlic cloves, sliced

a handful of fresh flat-leaf
  parsley, roughly torn

150 ml (¼ pint) olive oil

2.5 kg (5½ lb) large onions,
  sliced

1 celery stalk, diced

1 carrot, diced

1 rosemary branch, 2 bay leaves
  and 2 sage leaves, tied together
  to make a bouquet garni

200 ml (7 fl oz) white wine

salt and freshly ground black
  pepper

Place the veal joint on a chopping board and with a sharp knife unroll it until you obtain a long, flat piece, skin-side down. Season with salt and pepper, rubbing them well into the meat, followed by the garlic and parsley. Roll up again and tie together with 4 pieces of string, trimming off any excess.

Heat the olive oil in a large saucepan, add the veal and seal on all sides. Remove from the pan and set aside. Add the onions, celery and carrot to the pan, season with salt and pepper and stir well. Add the bouquet garni and cook until the onions begin to soften. Put the meat back in the pan, cover with a lid, then reduce the heat to low and cook for 3 hours, until very tender. Check from time to time that it isn't sticking to the pan, stirring the onions and turning the meat. After 3 hours, raise the heat, add the wine and simmer for 5 minutes. Remove the meat from the pan and set aside. With a potato masher, mash the onions slightly. Taste and adjust the seasoning,

Serve the onion sauce with some cooked pennette pasta and freshly grated Parmesan. For the main course, slice the veal and serve with a little of the sauce and a green salad.

PASSIONE

# polpette al vapore

## steamed meatballs

This dish has great sentimental value for me, as my mother would cook it when I was recovering from an illness. Because the meatballs are steamed and not fried, they are gentle on the stomach and easy to digest. It's a good way to enjoy meatballs without the added fat! Use the best lean minced beef you can find; minced steak is ideal.

**serves 4–6**

2 tablespoons extra virgin olive oil

3 tablespoons water

500 g (1 lb 2 oz) very lean minced beef

2 garlic cloves, very finely chopped

a handful of fresh flat-leaf parsley, very finely chopped

salt and freshly ground black pepper

Half fill a pan with water and put it on the hob to boil. Cover with a plate roughly the same size as the pan, or just a little larger, and put half the olive oil and the water on the plate.

Meanwhile, in a large bowl, mix together the beef, garlic, parsley, the remaining olive oil and some salt and pepper. It is much easier to do this with your hands. When all the ingredients are well combined, shape into about 25 small balls.

When the water begins to boil, turn down the heat to medium, so the water is gently simmering. Place the meatballs on the plate on top of the pan and cover with an upturned plate or, ideally, a glass bowl so that you can see though it. Leave to steam for 30 minutes, turning the meatballs over halfway through. Serve immediately, as the meat tends to toughen slightly when cool. You can serve the meatballs with pasta or on their own, with some good bread to mop up the liquid.

# il ragu

## stuffed beef rolls in tomato ragu

This recipe takes me back to my childhood Sunday lunches and, more recently, to family gatherings when I return to my home village. My Aunt Maria was the 'queen' of this dish and would spend the entire morning checking, stirring and making sure it was just right for all the family to enjoy. It is traditionally made every Sunday in all regions of southern Italy. It is a simple dish to prepare and takes about two hours to cook – some traditionalists will cook it for longer to get an even richer tomato sauce, but if you follow this recipe two hours will suffice. The tomato sauce is used to flavour pasta for the primo (pasta course) and the meat is eaten as a secondo (main course). Any leftover sauce can be used to flavour pasta dishes throughout the week.

PASSIONE

serves 6

12 small thin sirloin steaks

25 g (1 oz) Parmesan cheese,
    freshly grated

4 garlic cloves, finely chopped

a handful of fresh flat-leaf
    parsley, torn

salt and freshly ground black
    pepper

**for the sauce:**

6 tablespoons olive oil

150 ml (¼ pint) red wine

1 onion, very finely chopped

1 celery stalk, very finely chopped

2 tablespoons tomato concentrate
    or tomato purée, diluted in
    400 ml (14 fl oz) lukewarm
    water

2 x 400 g tins of chopped
    tomatoes

a handful of fresh basil leaves,
    torn

Arrange the slices of meat on a chopping board or a clean work surface and flatten them with a meat tenderiser (if you don't have one, place a flat wooden spatula over the meat and bash with the palm of your hand). Season with salt and pepper, then sprinkle with the grated Parmesan, garlic and parsley. Roll each slice up tightly and secure well with toothpicks.

For the sauce, heat the olive oil in a large saucepan. When hot, lower the heat, add the meat rolls and seal well on all sides. Increase the heat again, add the wine and simmer until it has reduced by half. Remove the meat and set aside.

Add the onion and celery to the pan and stir well. Cook until the remainder of the wine has nearly evaporated, then put the meat back in the pan and pour over the diluted tomato concentrate and the chopped tomatoes. Season with salt and pepper and stir in the basil. Lower the heat and cover with a lid, but not completely, so some of the steam can escape. Cook gently for 2 hours, stirring from time to time. Check the seasoning.

Serve the tomato sauce with some cooked pasta such as tagliatelle or large rigatoni. Then serve the meat rolls as a main course with a green salad.

# cotolette di agnello alla griglia ripiene di prosciutto ed erbe

grilled lamb cutlets filled with Parma ham and herbs

You can make the filling in advance, or make lots of it and store some in the fridge or freezer for another time. When choosing lamb cutlets, go to a reliable butcher and ask for organic (if available) or the best-quality racks of lamb. Usually one rack of lamb contains approximately six cutlets.

**serves 4**

12 lamb cutlets

salt and freshly ground black
   pepper

**for the filling:**

10 fresh sage leaves

a handful of fresh rosemary
   needles

a handful of fresh flat-leaf
   parsley leaves

a handful of fresh basil leaves

1 garlic clove, finely chopped

6 tablespoons freshly grated
   Parmesan cheese

100 g (4 oz) butter, slightly
   softened (remove from the
   fridge about an hour in
   advance)

6 slices of Parma ham

Place all the herbs on a chopping board and chop very finely together. Place them in a bowl with the garlic, Parmesan, butter and some salt and pepper and mix well until you get a smooth paste.

Arrange the Parma ham slices overlapping slightly on a piece of clingfilm and spread the paste evenly over them with a spatula. Then, with the help of the clingfilm, roll up the ham into a sausage shape, encased in the clingfilm, and tie the ends so the filling doesn't escape. Place in the fridge for at least an hour.

Slice each lamb cutlet horizontally through the centre, leaving it joined at one end, and open it up like a butterfly. With a meat tenderiser, flatten each piece. You can ask your butcher to do this for you if you prefer.

Remove the filling from the fridge and discard the clingfilm. Cut the filling into 2.5 cm (1 inch) slices, pressing slightly so it becomes flat. Place on one side of each cutlet and fold the other side over the top. Press together well, making sure that none of the filling escapes. Transfer the cutlets to a baking tray lined with foil and season with salt and pepper. Place under a hot grill and grill for about 2 minutes on each side for rare, 4 minutes for medium or, for well done, as long as you like! Serve immediately with Patate Saltate (see page 138).

Every March my mother would set off first thing one morning to the market town of Salerno. She would return that afternoon with a beautiful little piglet slung on her back in a canvas sack, its head poking out over the top. It was a happy ritual for my mother to put the piglet down in the back garden among the gathered family. We would all admire her choice and engage in a heated debate about how big he was going to grow, how long it would take and how good the meat might be. My mother always allowed me to play with him for a short while before he was put in the pigpen. After the first day, though, I was barely allowed near him; he became my mother's baby.

The piglet would be castrated soon after he was brought home. The castrator, who toured the region's villages, called to do the deed. I was mesmerised by this strange character. He was an eerie presence, wandering through the village shouting, 'Fuoco, fuoco!' Fuoco means fire, but I never did learn why he chose that word to announce his menacing arrival. He carried an umbrella and a bag containing his knife. With his faithful dog always at his side, he would go from house to house offering his grisly services. For a small fee, he would take any animal, cut off its testicles with a single flash of his knife and flick them into the air for the dog to catch and eat.

After the castration, nobody but my mother went near the piglet for the rest of his short life. He was kept in a pen in the back garden, where she would care for him as if he were another child, talking to him and stroking him every day. If he was sick, she would even stay up all night with him. She kept him well fed on leftovers such as porridge and bread, mixed with animal feed to fatten him up. In addition to this, the piglet tucked away an incredible amount of vegetables — root vegetables, carrots, liquorice, fennel roots, plus acorns, chestnuts and herbs to give the meat some flavour. She was careful not to frighten him and certainly never hit him. He lived well and grew bigger every day.

The pig was killed in winter. It was a terrible time. Somehow the animal knew what was going to happen, and the night before the slaughter he would cry and scream all night. It was heartbreaking.

In the morning, my mother would go out, give him a last meal and sit with him for a while. After she had said her silent farewell, it all happened very quickly. With lightening speed, my father, with two or three friends to help, would have the pig tied securely by his hind legs on a long table. His throat was cut instantly and the blood was collected in a bowl ready to be cooked with onions and bay leaves as a delicacy.

It was an occasion of great excitement for a boy of my age. I used to invite my friends in to witness the blood-thirsty drama of the kill and to share the feast that followed. My mother never took part in the slaughter, but stood and watched to make sure the men were not too rough with the poor beast. I never saw her shed a tear, but she told me later that she loved every one of those animals and was crying inside. She explained that she never let herself forget that the pig was food for her family.

No part of the pig was wasted; the blood was collected and the meat was hung. Boiling water was poured over the skin and the hairs scraped off, leaving an average of 130 kilos of pork to be eaten fresh or made into salami and sausages.

PASSIONE

# porchetta

stuffed rolled pork belly

Traditionally in Italy, porchetta is a whole piglet filled with lots of fresh herbs and slow-roasted either in a wood oven or outdoors on a spit. It is made at home or sold ready-made as a takeaway, and you can buy it whole, a few slices or just have a slice between bread as a sandwich. As whole piglets are not that easily obtainable, I use pork belly and the result is the same. It is simple to prepare and can be made in advance and eaten cold – a good idea for parties or to feed a large group of people for Sunday lunch.

PASSIONE

serves 10–12

5 kg (11 lb) piece of pork belly –
   ask the butcher to remove the
   ribs and trim off the excess fat
25 g (1 oz) coarse salt
leaves from a large bunch of fresh
   thyme
needles from a large bunch of
   fresh rosemary, roughly
   chopped
a large bunch of fresh sage
   leaves, roughly chopped
1 tablespoon fennel seeds (if you
   are lucky enough to find wild
   fennel, use it instead, finely
   chopped – its flavour is unique)
8 garlic cloves, finely chopped
2 tablespoons olive oil
6 tablespoons runny honey
coarsely ground black pepper

Preheat the oven to its highest setting. Lay the pork belly skin-side down. Sprinkle half the salt and lots of coarsely ground black pepper over it, rubbing them well into the meat with your fingers. Leave to rest for 10 minutes so the salt and pepper settle well into the meat. Then sprinkle the herbs, fennel seeds and garlic evenly all over it.

Next tie up the meat. You will need 10 pieces of string, each about 30 cm (12 inches) long. Carefully roll the meat up width-ways and tie it very tightly with string in the middle of the joint. Then tie at either end about 1 cm (½ inch) from the edge and keep tying along the joint until you have used up all the string. The filling should be well wrapped – if any excess filling escapes from the sides, push it in. With your hands, massage 1 tablespoon of the olive oil all over the joint. Then rub the remaining salt and some more black pepper over it. Grease a large roasting tin with the remaining olive oil and place the pork in it. Roast for 10 minutes, then turn it over. After 15 minutes, reduce the oven temperature to 150°C (300°F, Gas Mark 2) and cover the meat with alumini-um foil. (If you like the crackling very crisp, don't bother with the foil, but remember that the porchetta needs to be sliced thinly and crispy crackling will make this difficult.) Roast for 3 hours.

Remove the joint from the oven and coat with the honey, drizzling some of the juices from the roasting tin all over it too. Insert a fork in either side of the joint and lift it on to a wooden board. If you are serving the porchetta immediately, place the roasting tin on the hob and stir with a wooden spoon, scraping up all the caramelised bits from the base of the tin, until the juices from the meat reduce and thicken slightly. Slice the joint thinly and serve with the sauce. Alternatively, leave the meat to cool and slice when needed. It will keep for up to a week in the fridge.

# polletto in agrodolce

baby chicken in a cider vinegar sauce

Baby chickens (poussins) are much more tender than a fully matured one. They also look more attractive when serving. You can choose whether to serve a whole one or half per person, depending on people's appetite. If you are serving a starter and accompaniments, then one poussin between two people is sufficient.

**serves 2–4**

2 baby chickens (poussins), boned (ask your butcher to do this for you)

6 tablespoons olive oil

salt and freshly ground black pepper

**for the filling:**

2 garlic cloves, peeled

2 tablespoons capers

1 teaspoon sea salt

2 teaspoons extra virgin olive oil

freshly ground black pepper

**for the sauce:**

2 garlic cloves, peeled

needles from 2 branches of fresh rosemary

120 ml (4 fl oz) white wine

120 ml (4 fl oz) cider vinegar

First make the filling by placing all the ingredients in a mortar and pounding them with a pestle until you obtain a pulp.

Open up each poussin like a butterfly and lay skin-side down on a chopping board. Spread the filling evenly over the flesh side, then fold the poussin back over and secure the opening with wooden toothpicks, weaving them in and out. Season all over with salt and pepper. Heat the olive oil in a large frying pan, add the poussins, then reduce the heat slightly and cook until golden brown on all sides. Cover the pan and cook gently for 20 minutes.

Meanwhile, make the sauce. Place the garlic and rosemary in a mortar and pound with a pestle. Add the wine and cider vinegar and mix well.

Raise the heat under the poussins, add the sauce and simmer until reduced by half, stirring all the time. Arrange the poussins on a plate and pour over the sauce. Serve immediately.

PASSIONE

# petti di pollo con limone e timo

chicken breasts with lemon and thyme

Oh, the taste of my childhood: chickens scratching in the back yard, lemons and thyme from the garden! A distant but very vivid memory. Try this recipe with free-range or corn-fed chicken breasts – the combination with lemon and fresh thyme is wonderful. Serve with boiled new potatoes and green beans.

**serves 4**

150 ml (¼ pint) white wine

juice of 1 lemon

4 boneless chicken breasts

plain flour, for dusting

120 ml (4 fl oz) olive oil

2 small onions, finely sliced

1 lemon, zest and pith removed, thinly sliced, plus a few lemon slices to garnish

16 branches of fresh thyme, plus a few sprigs to garnish

10 fresh sage leaves

salt and freshly ground black pepper

In a small bowl, mix together the wine and lemon juice, then set aside.

Season the chicken breasts with salt and pepper and rub well in. Lightly dust them with some flour, shaking off any excess. With the palm of your hand, flatten the breasts slightly. Heat the olive oil in a large pan. Add the chicken and seal on both sides (some chicken breasts contain water and may spit while cooking – to prevent this, cover with a lid). Once they are well sealed and golden brown, remove the chicken breasts from the pan and set aside. Lower the heat, add the onions, season with salt and pepper and sweat until the onions are soft. Add the lemon slices, thyme and sage leaves and mix well. Return the chicken to the pan, cover and cook over a gentle heat for 3 minutes.

Raise the heat (but be careful not to burn the onions and lemon), add the wine and lemon juice mixture, then cover and cook for 10–15 seconds, until the mixture is bubbling. Remove the lid and simmer until the liquid has evaporated slightly – you will see the sauce thickening. Taste and adjust the seasoning if necessary.

Arrange the chicken breasts on a large plate or on individual serving plates and pour the sauce over. Garnish with lemon slices and sprigs of thyme.

# bocconcini di pollo con aceto alle mele

chicken bites wrapped in pancetta and sage with a cider vinegar dressing

This recipe came out of the blue when I was making a chicken dish for some guests at home. As usual, I had bought too much food and was left with a couple of chicken breasts. In the fridge I found pancetta and fresh sage, so I decided to put these ingredients together with a tangy cider vinegar dressing and made these delicious bocconcini, which I served with pre-dinner drinks. They make an excellent starter. Alternatively, you can make lots of them in advance for parties or as snacks with drinks. If you serve them cold like this, don't pour the dressing over as they will go soggy. Arrange the bocconcini on plates garnished with some salad leaves and put the dressing in small bowls for dipping.

**serves 4 as a starter**

2 skinless, boneless chicken breasts

6 very thin slices of pancetta, cut in half

12 fresh sage leaves

2 tablespoons olive oil

a few salad leaves, to serve

**for the dressing:**

120 ml (4 fl oz) extra virgin olive oil

4 tablespoons cider vinegar

1 teaspoon finely chopped fresh parsley

salt and freshly ground black pepper

Cut the chicken breasts lengthways in half and cut each half into 3 chunks. Lay the half slices of pancetta on a clean work surface, place a sage leaf on top of each one and wrap them around the chicken chunks.

Heat the olive oil in a frying pan over a medium heat, add the pancetta-wrapped chicken and seal all over, taking care not to burn the pancetta. Turn the heat down and, with the help of 2 forks, keep turning the bocconcini until the chicken has cooked through. This should take about 10 minutes.

Meanwhile, make the dressing. Place all the ingredients in a small bowl and whisk with a fork until it begins to thicken slightly.

Remove the bocconcini from the frying pan and drain on kitchen paper to remove excess oil. Arrange on a plate with some salad leaves and pour the dressing over. Serve immediately.

PASSIONE

I have always loved animals. My father kept cats and dogs and I grew up surrounded by a whole range of farmyard creatures, which became my play-mates. But I soon learned not to become too attached to them.

Every Easter, my father would return from his travels laden with goodies for our traditional spring feast: the finest goat, chicken, capon and lamb, raised by his farmer friends. To make sure he was getting the freshest meat and the finest quality, he would make a point of seeing each animal alive before he bought it.

One year he made his mistake. A couple of weeks before Easter, he accept-ed a baby goat as payment for an old debt. It was just a few weeks old but he knew it would be perfect for our Easter lunch. He also thought it would be fun for me to have a baby goat to play with. To be fair to my father, he did tell me that it was our Easter lunch, but I was just a small child and really didn't want to believe such a brutal truth, so I pushed it to the back of my mind.

Looking after this hungry kid was a 24-hour-a-day job. I called him Bottiglia (Bottle) because I fed him milk from a bottle. He quickly became my whole life. My family and friends teased me mercilessly but I loved him. Bottiglia was my friend, constant companion and confidant. I created a wonderful adventure dream world in my head for the two of us. He came with me to the beach, trotted behind me on my jaunts to the mountains and wandered through the village streets with me. He was my little shadow, and I believe he loved me as much as I loved him. I was his surrogate mother and he was my pride and joy.

It came to school time and I kicked up a fuss. I didn't want to leave my new best friend at home but my parents threatened me, saying that if I didn't go to school they would take him away. For two weeks I went to school every day without fail and without complaint. I didn't want to lose Bottiglia.

The day before Easter, I ran home from school and straight through the house to find him. I had been thinking all day about Bottiglia and the adventures we could have. I was so looking forward to seeing him ... and there he was, hanging by his back legs from the ceiling, his throat cut and blood still dripping from his neck. I couldn't believe the horror in front of my eyes. Even now, it still counts as the worst day of my life. I started to cry, and my mother shouted at my father, telling him he shouldn't have done it, knowing how much I loved the goat. My father would have none of it. As far as he was concerned, he had done nothing wrong. He walloped me for crying and said I was old enough to know better than to get attached to food.

The next day at lunch I felt sick. I couldn't eat my friend but I had to sit and watch everyone else tucking in. I'll never forget my little sister laughing at me, and the rest of the table joining in.

Although this might seem harsh, ultimately my father was right. The kid was always intended as our Easter meal. It was a valuable lesson. From that moment, I still loved animals but I also respected them as a source of food.

# oca (o anitra) arrosto con mele e castagne in vino rosso

roast goose (or duck) with apples and chestnuts in red wine

**This should really be cooked for a special occasion, such as Christmas. It takes a little time to prepare but the result is well worth it. Goose and duck are rich, fatty meats so they need something sharp and acidic like apples to counteract this.**

**serves 6–8**

1 goose, weighing about 4–5 kg
 (9–11 lb), or 1 duck, weighing
 about 2.5 kg (5½ lb)

4 slices of pancetta

6 tablespoons olive oil

1 glass of red wine

4 carrots, cut lengthways in half

salt and freshly ground black
 pepper

First make the stuffing. Heat the olive oil in a large frying pan and sauté the pancetta and onion for a minute. Then add the giblets and continue to sauté until all the ingredients have softened. Add the herbs and garlic and season with black pepper. Stir in the apples, chestnuts, bread and sweet wine and continue to cook for a couple of minutes, then remove from the heat.

Take the goose or duck and slide your fingers under the skin at the neck end, gently separating it from the flesh. With the help of a flat wooden spatula, lay slices of pancetta between the skin and flesh. If you accidentally break the skin, just cover up the tear with another slice of pancetta. Pull the skin over the neck opening from both sides to close it and then turn the bird upside down. Season the cavity with salt and pepper and fill with the stuffing, securing either side with wooden toothpicks so the filling does not escape. Truss up the whole bird with string, so the legs and wings are tightly secured, then rub it all over with salt and pepper.

Preheat the oven to 180°C (350°F, Gas Mark 4). Heat the olive oil in a large roasting tin on the hob. Put the bird in the tin and seal well all over, then remove from the heat and add the wine. Be careful to move away when you do this because, with the intense heat and the fat from the bird, it may set alight. If this happens, don't worry; the fire should extinguish itself quickly. Remove the bird from the tin, pour out the liquid and set it

**for the stuffing:**

2 tablespoons olive oil

100 g (4 oz) pancetta, cubed

1 large onion, roughly chopped

giblets from the bird (remove the
fat), roughly chopped

a few sprigs of fresh thyme,
rosemary and sage, finely
chopped

2 garlic cloves, finely chopped

2 eating apples, cored and cut
into cubes

15 cooked chestnuts, left whole

50 g (2 oz) stale bread, soaked in
a glass of white wine to soften,
then roughly chopped

100 ml (3½ fl oz) sweet white
wine (e.g. Sauternes)

**for the apples and chestnuts:**

3–4 eating apples, peeled, cored
and halved

250 g (9 oz) cooked chestnuts

75 ml (3 fl oz) red wine

a knob of butter

aside. Line the bottom of the tin with the carrots, arranging them in 2 lines like a railway track. Place the bird on top of the carrots (they prevent it sticking to the tin). If necessary, use more carrots for extra support! Pour in a glass of water, cover with aluminium foil and roast for 3–4 hours for a goose, depending on the size, or 2 hours for a duck. To check if the bird is properly cooked, insert a skewer between the breast and the leg; if the juices run clear, it is done.

After the bird has been cooking for about 40 minutes, add another glass of water to the roasting tin, and then again 40–50 minutes after that. About 10 minutes before the end of the cooking time, remove the foil and baste the bird with the juices. Remove from the oven and leave to rest for 5–10 minutes before carving.

Meanwhile, for the apples and chestnuts, heat half the liquid set aside earlier in a large frying pan. Add the apples and chestnuts and sauté until browned on each side. Add the remaining liquid and let it bubble until evaporated. Remove from the heat and pour out excess fat. Place the pan back on the heat, pour in the red wine and simmer until almost completely evaporated. Stir in a knob of butter and see the sauce thicken.

Carve the bird and serve immediately with the apples and chestnuts.

# petti d'anatra in limoncello

duck breasts in limoncello

**Limoncello is a lemon liqueur made on the Amalfi coast, near my home. When I was a child it used to be home-made only, but now it has become quite an industry and is sold world-wide. It is a very pure liqueur, made solely from lemons, sugar and alcohol. The citrus/sweet flavour goes very well with duck. Serve this dish with a purée of root vegetables such as carrot and celeriac.**

**serves 4**

4 boneless duck breasts

2 large lemons

250 ml (8 fl oz) limoncello

50 g (2 oz) butter

2 tablespoons olive oil

salt and freshly ground black
   pepper

Pat the duck breasts dry and place them in a shallow dish. Peel the lemons with a potato peeler so you get ringlets of lemon zest, then squeeze the juice from them. Scatter the lemon ringlets over the duck, pour over the juice and limoncello and leave to marinate for about 30 minutes.

Remove the duck from the marinade, dry on kitchen paper and season well all over with salt and pepper. Do not discard the marinade.

Clarify the butter in a large frying pan by letting it melt, then when it begins to foam, carefully lifting off the foam with a tablespoon, leaving just the clear, golden liquid. Add the olive oil. When it is hot, place the duck breasts in the pan, skin-side down, and seal well on both sides. Reduce the heat and cook for about 12 minutes, turning the duck over from time to time. This will give you medium-cooked duck, which I think is ideal for this dish. Now turn the heat up high, pour in the marinade and let it evaporate, turning the duck over and giving the pan a shake from time to time – this will help the sauce thicken.

As soon as the sauce has thickened, remove the pan from the heat and place the duck breasts on a chopping board. Leave to rest for about 5 minutes, then cut them into slices, arrange on 4 plates or one serving dish and pour over the sauce. Serve immediately.

PASSIONE

# petto di faraona ripieno di erbe con salsa al balsamico

breast of guinea fowl stuffed with herbs and served with a balsamic sauce

This is an old recipe from the Naples region, traditionally made with pig's spleen. Spleen is no longer commonly available and probably a little offputting to a lot of people, so I have used guinea fowl breasts instead. If you prefer, you can use chicken.

**serves 4**

4 boneless guinea fowl breasts

6 tablespoons olive oil

150 ml (¼ pint) balsamic vinegar

150 ml (¼ pint) red wine vinegar

275 ml (9 fl oz) red wine

salt and freshly ground black
    pepper

**for the stuffing:**

100 g (4 oz) softened butter

4 garlic cloves, squashed and
    finely chopped

1 red chilli, finely chopped

50 g (2 oz) fresh mint, finely
    chopped

50 g (2 oz) fresh flat-leaf parsley,
    finely chopped

First make the stuffing. Put the butter, garlic, chilli, mint and parsley in a bowl and mix together until smooth, adding a little salt to taste. Shape into a ball, wrap in clingfilm and put in the fridge until ready to use.

Place the guinea fowl breasts on a chopping board, skin-side down. Make a small pocket in each one with a sharp knife and fill with the herb butter. Fold over the skin from both sides to cover the flesh and secure it with wooden toothpicks, weaving them in and out. Ensure that none of the filling comes out.

Heat the olive oil in a large saucepan, add the guinea fowl breasts and cook until sealed on all sides. Pour in the balsamic vinegar, red wine vinegar and wine, turn down the heat and cook for 20 minutes, turning the guinea fowl over half way through. Remove the guinea fowl from the pan and leave to cool. Take the saucepan off the heat and beat with a whisk until the sauce begins to thicken and has an almost creamy consistency. Taste and adjust the seasoning if necessary.

Remove the toothpicks from the guinea fowl and slice. Arrange the slices on a plate and pour the sauce over.

# faraona con pancetta e uva passa

guinea fowl with pancetta and raisins

The sweetness of raisins goes well with guinea fowl – although you could substitute chicken if you prefer. You could also buy ready-cut guinea fowl pieces rather than jointing a whole bird, but I do recommend that you use the legs, as they enhance the flavour of the dish. Smoked streaky bacon can be substituted for the pancetta.

**serves 4**

1 x 1 kg (2¼ lb) guinea fowl, jointed into 4 (you could ask your butcher to do this)

75 g (3 oz) plain flour

4 tablespoons olive oil

100 g (4 oz) pancetta, cut into thin strips

10 garlic cloves

100 g (4 oz) raisins

2 sprigs of fresh rosemary

1 glass of white wine

1 glass of chicken stock

salt and freshly ground black pepper

Preheat the oven to 150°C (300°F, Gas Mark 2). Coat the guinea fowl pieces in the flour, shaking off any excess. Heat the olive oil in a large casserole, add the pancetta and fry until browned. Remove the pancetta from the pan and set aside.

Place the guinea fowl in the pan and cook until sealed on all sides. Add the unpeeled garlic cloves, raisins, rosemary and wine. Simmer until the wine has reduced by half, then add the stock and return the pancetta to the pan. Cover tightly with a lid, transfer to the oven and cook for 30–40 minutes, until the guinea fowl is tender. Taste the sauce and adjust the seasoning, then serve.

When I came to England at the end of the Sixties, there were two things I wanted: a pair of Levis and a gun. I had been out hunting with my father on Sunday mornings since I was tiny. Our family had hunted for at least two generations, so it was in my blood. When I was a small boy, I was effectively the dog! I would run through the undergrowth and frighten the birds out. When my father

was about to shoot, he would shout, '*Hop!*', which meant, 'Don't move!', and I would duck down. At 11 o'clock we would head back to the village to go to church. My father would leave his gun and pack of game outside. It would be full of blackbirds, wood pigeons, sparrows and quails.

I remember how strict my father was about his gun. I was never allowed to touch it. He always prepared and stored the cartridges at my grandfather's house and the gun at ours. He frightened me with stories of accidents and injuries, so I was always very careful. He usually let me have a couple of shots with his sixteen-bore at the end of a day's hunting, though.

I bought my gun and Levis almost as soon as I got to England. Then I found there was nowhere to shoot. I spent days going round the countryside asking farmers if I could shoot on their land. Eventually one took pity on me and allowed me on his property, as long as I stuck to wood pigeons and rabbits. There is quite a large hunting fraternity in England, which I was lucky enough to join, and I used to go hunting frequently. These days, if friends ask me to join them, I gladly go along.

*San Nicola, a disused monastery on the hills of Minori (left): out hunting with a farmer's son (above)*

# coniglio con aglio e rosmarino servito con bruschetta

rabbit with garlic and rosemary served with bruschetta

Rabbit is cooked all over Italy in different ways and the method I have given here is the way we cook it at home. It was always my son Christopher's favourite dish at Sunday lunches and I dedicate this recipe to him. If you don't like rabbit, you can cook chicken, guinea fowl or turkey in exactly the same way. Use good extra virgin olive oil for this recipe, as you need quite a lot and the flavour really comes out.

PASSIONE

serves 4

1 rabbit, chopped into medium-
sized chunks on the bone
(including the liver, kidneys and
ribs), or use ready-prepared
boneless chunks of rabbit

plain flour for dusting

150 ml (¼ pint) extra virgin
olive oil

cloves from 1 garlic head, kept
whole with skins on

a large bunch of fresh rosemary,
broken in half

150 ml (¼ pint) white wine

salt and freshly ground black
pepper

for the bruschetta:

a few slices of bread

a few garlic cloves, peeled but left
whole

Season the rabbit with salt and pepper and dust with the flour. Heat the extra virgin olive oil in a large, heavy-based frying pan. When hot, add the floured rabbit chunks and seal well on all sides until golden brown and quite crisp. Reduce the heat, add the garlic and rosemary, cover with a lid and cook gently for 30 minutes, turning the pieces of rabbit from time to time. Raise the heat to high, remove the lid, add the wine and simmer until it has evaporated.

When the rabbit is ready, make the bruschetta. Toast some slices of bread, immediately rub them with the garlic and then drizzle with some of the olive oil that will have risen to the top of the rabbit sauce. Serve the rabbit accompanied by the bruschetta.

## preserved meats

**Preserved meats are extremely popular throughout Italy, with each region having its own specialities. Although pig is the most common animal from which preserved meats are made, wild boar, goose and beef are also used.**

### Bresaola

Bresaola is air-dried beef. It is a popular antipasto on many Italian restaurant menus and can also be found ready-sliced in packets in most supermarkets, although this variety is very 'plastic' and tastes nothing like the original. My friend, Mauro Bregoli, who lives in the New Forest, is a master of curing and preserving meat, and his smoked bresaola is exceptional. Whenever I put bresaola on the menu at passione, I order his. The best-quality bresaola can be found at good Italian delicatessens and you should ask for the *punta d'anca*, which is the fleshiest and most succulent part.

Bresaola should be served thinly sliced, drizzled with some extra virgin olive oil and lemon juice, and accompanied with some rocket and shavings of Parmesan cheese or with warm caprino (mild Italian goat's cheese).

### Cotechino and zampone

These are both a type of huge sausage. Cotechino is a mixture of pork rind, fat and meat, all minced up and very finely seasoned with spices, then placed inside sausage skins and cooked for a long time. Zampone is a pig's trotter minced up with pork rind, back fat, lean meat and some spices and seasoning and then placed in a sausage skin.

Both are now made commercially and sold in vacuum packs, which you cook in boiling water at home. They are traditionally served at New Year with stewed lentils. The descriptions of both may sound a little off-putting, but I guarantee that if you like sausages, these are the best! They are easily obtainable at Italian delis. Serve with stewed lentils or mashed potatoes and braised cabbage for a filling winter meal.

### Prosciutto crudo di Parma

Made from pigs raised in the Emilia Romagna region, this is probably Italy's most renowned cured ham. Other regions have their own versions – for example, San Daniele from Friuli and San Leo from Marche. The best-quality hams are cured on the bone for at least 18–24 months. Parma ham is traditionally served as part of an antipasto with other cured meats, pickles and preserved vegetables (see page 161). See also Antipasto di Pesche e Prosciutto Crudo di Parma on page 103.

## Salami

Italy has a vast variety of salami, which are mostly commercially produced nowadays, although many farmers and local *salumerie* still make their own in the old-fashioned way. Good salami is made with *suino* (pure lard), and the regional varieties have their own flavourings, such as black peppercorns, fennel seeds, chilli and red wine. Some of the most common varieties of salami found in delis in this country are Milano, Napoletano, Felino, Cacciatorino, Soppressata, Finocchiona and Calabrese, each of which has its own characteristics. I suggest you try a few slices of each before picking your favourite. Serve a selection of salami as part of an antipasto, with pickles and preserved vegetables (see page 161).

## Sausages

There is a wide range of Italian sausages available in good delicatessens. Most are pork-based, with flavourings such as fennel seeds, rosemary, sage and chilli. They are usually short and fat, tied with string, and sold loosely from the cold counter. Italian sausages are delicious grilled or fried, as you would other sausages, or added to a thick tomato ragu (see page 171) to make a filling pasta sauce.

There is also the luganega sausage, which is a very long pork sausage, common in northern Italy, usually sold by the metre. Buy a long piece and wrap it round in a spiral shape (like the English Cumberland sausage), secure it with toothpicks and fry it, adding rosemary sprigs and finishing off with red wine. This is delicious eaten with polenta or mashed potatoes.

# verdure vegetables

**S**outhern Italians love vegetables so much that Neapolitans used to be known as *mangiafoglie*, or leaf-eaters. To this day, Italians have a rich tradition of vegetable cookery and serve vegetables as main course dishes, not just starters and accompaniments.

When I was growing up, we usually ate meat only once or twice a week but we enjoyed an excellent, varied diet of seasonal vegetables. Nowadays, we can eat any vegetable all year round, but I miss the anticipation and excitement we felt at the beginning of each new season.

We knew we couldn't rely on fresh vegetables all year round, so right from the very first crop of spring we would start preserving them for the winter months.

It was a joy eating the vegetables we had preserved from spring and summer – not just for the taste but also for the memories. Every time I opened a new jar, it reminded me of the day I had filled it. It may have been a feast day, or the first day of summer, or even a sad day, but the memories always came flooding back. Sometimes the taste of those preserved vegetables was out of this world. Preserved aubergines, in particular, were so good that it was a miracle if they made it through to the winter months.

*Papá with his friend the chef Alfonso returning from Maiori market*

Winter was a joy for me in many ways. I loved the beautiful chestnuts, the dried figs and fruit, and the pungent flavours of preserved summer vegetables. But, after a long winter living on root vegetables and preserved vegetables, spring was really something to look forward to. It brought the first broad beans, peas, courgettes, chicory, cucumbers, onions, asparagus and endless salads.

There was always a big family feast to celebrate the arrival of spring and the new crop of small, succulent vegetables. We hadn't tasted fresh, young produce all winter. My father would cook a beautiful soup of broad beans, peas and pasta. We savoured the taste of the first spring salads, the little carrots and courgette flowers.

The greengrocer shops gradually came alive with colour as they filled with new produce. As spring continued, more and more vegetables arrived – all kinds of cabbages, large aubergines and tomatoes. Then, with the summer, came an abundance of vegetables and the first fruit crops of the season. It was magnificent. Small pears and figs straight from the trees, herbs, chillies, peppers – everything was available and everything was delicious.

# puré di ceci

chickpea purée

**Try this purée of chickpeas as an alternative to potatoes or other root vegetables. It makes a wonderful accompaniment to meat dishes, such as Faraona con Pancetta e Uva Passa (see page 127).**

**serves 4-6**

4 tablespoons olive oil

1 celery stalk, finely chopped

½ leek, finely chopped

1 onion, finely chopped

2 small carrots, finely chopped

a few rosemary needles

250 g (9 oz) dried chickpeas, soaked overnight in cold water and then drained

1 litre (1¾ pints) vegetable stock

salt and freshly ground black pepper

Heat the olive oil in a large saucepan, add the vegetables and rosemary and sweat until softened. Stir in the chickpeas, then add the stock. Bring to the boil, reduce the heat, then cover the pan and simmer for about 1½ hours, until the chickpeas are tender and have absorbed almost all the liquid.

Remove from the heat, place in a food processor or blender and whiz until smooth. Taste and adjust the seasoning. Serve immediately, or make in advance and then heat through gently just before serving.

# patate saltate

## sautéed potatoes

These are an essential accompaniment to all sorts of meat dishes and roasts. Leave the garlic cloves unpeeled and don't worry about the skin; it all adds to the flavour and appearance of the dish.

**serves 4**

400 g (14 oz) small new potatoes, scrubbed and cut in half

6 tablespoons olive oil

8 garlic cloves, unpeeled and squashed with the back of a knife

4 sprigs of fresh rosemary

salt and freshly ground black pepper

Cook the potatoes in boiling salted water until tender, then drain. Heat the olive oil in a frying pan and add the garlic and rosemary, followed by the potatoes. Allow to colour on all sides over a fairly high heat, stirring now and again to prevent them sticking to the pan. Season with salt and pepper and serve immediately.

# insalata di patate

## warm potato salad

For maximum flavour, it is imperative that this dish is served when the potatoes are still warm, so make sure that all the other ingredients are ready as soon as the potatoes are cooked. It makes an ideal accompaniment to Involtini di Pesce Spada con Finocchio (see page 88) for a light *al fresco* lunch.

**serves 4**

8 medium new potatoes

2 medium red onions, very finely sliced

1 tablespoon dried oregano

120 ml (4 fl oz) extra virgin olive oil

4 tablespoons red wine vinegar

salt and freshly ground black pepper

Wash and scrub the potatoes well but don't peel them. Cook in lightly salted boiling water until tender. Drain and remove the skins, holding the potatoes with a cloth to avoid burning your fingers (unless you have asbestos fingers like me!).

Cut the potatoes into quarters and place in a bowl with all the remaining ingredients. Mix well and serve immediately.

# tortino di patate e cavolo nero

potato and cavolo nero bake

Potatoes, cabbage and Taleggio cheese are a typically northern Italian combination. The climate is much cooler in the North and you would expect to eat such a dish there during winter. I have used cavolo nero in this recipe, as I find it much tastier, but you could use Savoy cabbage instead. Cavolo nero is grown mainly in Tuscany and has become widely available in supermarkets throughout the UK. Its name means 'black cabbage', referring to its long, thin leaves, which are so dark that they look almost black. It certainly stands out from the usual variety of cabbage found in greengrocer's.

Taleggio gives the dish a rich, creamy taste but if you can't find it, substitute fontina or a mature Cheddar.

If you cook this in four individual terracotta dishes, it makes an ideal vegetarian main course, served with a simple green salad. Prepare it in advance and then bake once your guests have arrived.

PASSIONE

**serves 4**

675 g (1½ lb) cavolo nero
  (large leaves only)

8 medium potatoes, peeled and
  thinly sliced

150 g (5 oz) butter

325 g (11 oz) Taleggio cheese,
  thinly sliced

salt and freshly ground black
  pepper

Remove the stalks and hard central core from the cavolo nero leaves and cook in plenty of boiling salted water for 3–5 minutes, until just tender but still slightly crisp. Drain well, place in cold water and then drain again, squeezing out any excess water with your hands. Dry on a kitchen cloth. Cook the potato slices in lightly salted boiling water for 3 minutes, then drain, place in cold water, drain again and dry well on a kitchen cloth.

Preheat the oven to its highest setting. To make individual servings, you will need 4 terracotta dishes about 20 cm (8 inches) in diameter and 3 cm (1¼ inches) deep. Grease each dish generously with some of the butter. Arrange half the potato slices, slightly overlapping, over the bottom of the dishes, dot with some of the butter and season with salt and pepper. Arrange the cavolo nero leaves over the potatoes, with the larger part of the leaf hanging a quarter of the way over the edge of the dish. About 10 cabbage leaves should suffice for each dish. Arrange half the cheese on top of the cabbage and then season. Top with the remaining potatoes, then with the remaining cheese. Place a cabbage leaf in the middle and fold over the excess leaves, pressing gently with your fingers so that none of the other ingredients are visible, then dot with butter. If you are making one large bake, grease a large baking tray with plenty of butter and then layer the ingredients as above.

Cover with aluminium foil, place in the oven and bake for 25 minutes. Remove from the oven and carefully lift off the foil, taking care not to burn yourself with the steam. Serve straight from the baking tray, if you have made a large bake. If you have made individual portions, place a plate over each one and flip over. You should get a lovely layer of golden-brown potatoes on the top. Serve immediately.

# carciofi ripieni
## stuffed globe artichokes

Artichokes are very popular in Italy, especially in the South where they grow in abundance. In fact Italy is the largest producer of artichokes in the Mediterranean and a great number are exported as well as eaten locally. Just like chestnut sellers on street corners in England, we used to have artichoke vendors selling roasted artichokes. The smell was irresistible.

I love artichokes and cook them in a variety of ways – roasted, fried, steamed and in salads (see page 156). My favourite way of cooking the large globe artichokes is to stuff them and slow-cook them in a pot. Try this recipe; it's simple to prepare, makes a wonderful starter and looks very impressive when served – almost too lovely to eat! Remember to provide finger bowls, spare plates to hold the discarded leaves, and plenty of good bread to soak up the sauce.

PaSSione

**serves 4**

4 large globe artichokes

8 handfuls of fresh flat-leaf
   parsley, roughly torn

4 garlic gloves, thinly sliced

8 anchovy fillets

24 cherry tomatoes, quartered,
   or 4 medium-sized tomatoes,
   roughly chopped

4 teaspoons capers

8 green olives, sliced

about 1.5 litres (2½ pints)
   vegetable stock

8 tablespoons extra virgin olive
   oil, plus a little extra for
   drizzling

salt and freshly ground black
   pepper

With a small, sharp knife, remove the bottom outer leaves of each artichoke and cut off the stalk. Trim the base slightly so the bottom is flat and the artichoke can stand upright. With your fingers, gently open out the artichoke until you can see the hairy choke. With a small scoop or teaspoon, remove and discard the choke, which is inedible. Season the artichoke cavities with salt and pepper and fill each with a handful of parsley, 1 sliced garlic clove, 2 anchovy fillets, 6 cherry tomatoes, 1 teaspoon of capers and 2 sliced green olives, gently pressing all the ingredients in.

Put the stock in a large saucepan, then add the stuffed artichokes. Pack them in tightly so they don't wobble during cooking; if your pan is too big and there is space between them, fill the gap with a large potato. The stock should come three-quarters of the way up the artichokes, so if necessary add some more.

Pour 2 tablespoons of olive oil into each stuffed artichoke and cover with another handful of parsley. Bring to the boil, then reduce the heat, cover the pan and simmer for 1 hour or until the artichokes are tender; if you can pull out a central leaf easily, they are done.

Carefully lift out the artichokes with a large slotted spoon and place on individual serving plates, then gently open up the artichokes so the filling can be seen. Pour about ½ ladleful of the stock over each artichoke and drizzle with some extra virgin olive oil. Serve immediately, with lots of bread to dip into the sauce.

# peperoni ripieni

## stuffed baby peppers

For this recipe, try to use small peppers or, if you prefer, the small, sweet long peppers. If you use the latter, slit them lengthways and remove the seeds, then make the filling as below, except for the provolone which you should slice in strips and place over the top of the peppers. Bake these long peppers for 20 minutes only. If you can't find either type of pepper, use ordinary peppers and serve 1 per person.

**serves 4**

8 red or yellow baby peppers

2 large potatoes, boiled and
    mashed

75 g (3 oz) provolone cheese, cut
    into very small cubes

4 tablespoons freshly grated
    Parmesan cheese

1 egg

3 tablespoons finely chopped
    fresh chives

a little olive oil for drizzling

salt and freshly ground black
    pepper

Preheat the oven to 200°C (400°F, Gas Mark 6). Remove the stalks from the peppers and set aside. With a small, sharp knife, remove the white membrane and seeds from inside the peppers, taking care not to tear the flesh.

Mix together the mashed potatoes, provolone, Parmesan, egg, chives and some salt and pepper. Using a teaspoon, fill the peppers three-quarters full with the mixture and then put the stalks back in place, like a stopper. Pack the peppers tightly into an ovenproof dish, drizzle with olive oil and bake for about 30 minutes, until tender. Serve immediately with a good green salad. They are also delicious eaten cold.

PASSIONE

# agrodolce di peperoni

sweet and sour peppers

Sweet and sour flavours go extremely well with peppers. This dish can be served as a starter with lots of bread to mop up the delicious olive oil, or as a side dish to accompany meat and game. It is ideal for making in large quantities for parties, as it can be eaten cold.

PASSIONE

serves 2–4

6 tablespoons extra virgin olive
oil

1 large yellow pepper, deseeded
and cut into thick strips

1 large red pepper, deseeded
and cut into thick strips

3 anchovy fillets

2 garlic cloves, peeled but left
whole

6 black olives

1 tablespoon capers

1 tablespoon sugar

4 tablespoons white wine vinegar

salt and freshly ground black
pepper

Heat the olive oil in a large frying pan, add the peppers and cook until the skins are golden brown. Then add the anchovy fillets, garlic, olives and capers. Stir in the sugar, then add the vinegar and allow to evaporate. Cook on a medium heat for about 5 minutes, or until the peppers are tender. Season to taste and serve hot or cold.

# lattuga ripiena

braised stuffed Cos lettuce

My grandmother used to make this dish using escarole, which she grew in her garden. It was a good way of making one lettuce go further, and it was also a means of using up stale bread – nothing was ever thrown away. The stuffed lettuce can be kept for a few days and it tastes even better cold than hot.

serves 4–6

6 tablespoons olive oil

1 small onion, finely chopped

1 garlic clove, finely chopped

½ yellow pepper, finely chopped

1 tomato, roughly chopped

7 green olives, finely sliced

1 small aubergine, peeled and cut into small cubes

1 courgette, finely chopped

a bunch of fresh flat-leaf parsley, finely chopped

100 g (4 oz) stale bread, roughly chopped

75 g (3 oz) Parmesan cheese, freshly grated

2 eggs

1 large Cos lettuce, opened up gently and small central leaves removed

600 ml (1 pint) vegetable stock

2 tablespoons extra virgin olive oil

salt and freshly ground black pepper

Heat the olive oil in a large pan, add the onion, garlic, yellow pepper, tomato, olives, aubergine and courgette and cook, stirring, for 1 minute. Add the parsley and season with salt and pepper. Reduce the heat and sweat the vegetables until soft. Then remove from the heat and leave to cool.

Place the bread in a food processor or blender and whiz until you get very fine breadcrumbs. Add the breadcrumbs and Parmesan to the vegetables, together with the eggs. Mix until smooth and season with salt and pepper if required. Fill the Cos lettuce with this mixture and tie it tightly with string. You may need help for this – someone will need to hold the lettuce while you tie string round it several times. Stand the lettuce up and gently bang it on the work surface so the filling goes down well. Place it, lying down, in a large pan, add the stock and cover the pan. Bring to the boil, then reduce the heat and simmer gently for 40 minutes, checking from time to time to make sure the liquid has not evaporated – if necessary, add a little more stock or water. After the first 10 minutes, drizzle with the extra virgin olive oil. If the filling escapes, don't worry; just gently push it in with a wooden spatula.

The stuffed lettuce can be served hot or cold. Put it on a serving dish, untie and cut into slices. If serving hot, leave it to stand for 5 minutes before slicing.

# fagottini di zucchini

stuffed courgette parcels

This is a different and interesting way of using courgettes. They are simple enough to prepare, but allow yourself some time and you will find that once you get going they are fun to make. They look good, too, and make an ideal starter with some salad leaves or to serve with drinks. I am sure your guests will be intrigued to know how you got the filling in!

**serves 6 as a starter**

4 large courgettes

350 g (12 oz) ricotta cheese

200 g (7 oz) potatoes, boiled and mashed

5 tablespoons freshly grated Parmesan cheese

8–12 fresh sage leaves

8–12 thin slices of fontina cheese, about 4 cm (1½ inches) square (you could substitute mature Cheddar)

a little butter for greasing

salt and freshly ground black pepper

With a sharp knife, cut the courgettes lengthways into slices 5 mm (¼ inch) thick; you should get 4–6 slices from each courgette. Cook the courgette slices in plenty of lightly salted boiling water for about 2 minutes, until just tender, then remove and plunge into cold water. Drain and dry on a kitchen cloth.

Preheat the oven to 240°C (475°F, Gas Mark 9). In a large bowl, mix together the ricotta, mashed potatoes, Parmesan and some salt and pepper. Take 2 slices of courgette, place them on a clean, dry surface and shape them in a cross. Repeat with the rest of the courgette slices. With your fingers, shape the ricotta mixture into balls about the size of a pingpong ball (one for each courgette cross). Place a ball in the middle of each cross, place a sage leaf on top and then fold the strips of courgette over to make a parcel. Place a slice of fontina cheese on top and secure with a wooden toothpick.

Line a baking tray with foil or greaseproof paper and grease with some butter. Place the courgette parcels on the baking tray. (At this stage, you can refrigerate them and cook when needed.) Bake for 10–12 minutes, until golden. Remove the parcels from the oven, place on a serving dish and remove the toothpicks. Serve warm, with some salad leaves.

# fette di melanzane con crosta di parmigiano e polenta

aubergine slices with a Parmesan and polenta crust

This idea was given to me by Liz while we were making Involtini di Melanzane alla Parmigiana (see page 152) together one day. It was her grandmother's version of 'vegetarian steak', which she would make for the family during wartime when meat was scarce. It can be served as a snack, side dish or, indeed, a vegetarian main course. The aubergine slices are delicious topped with Salsa alla Crudaiola (see page 170), a little garlic, basil, salt and pepper, or with Vedure Miste Sott'Olio (see page 161).

serves 4–6

2 large eggs

25 g (1 oz) Parmesan cheese, freshly grated

1 large aubergine, peeled and cut lengthways into slices 5 mm (¼ inch) thick

plain flour seasoned with salt and pepper, for dusting

250 g (9 oz) polenta

7 tablespoons olive oil

salt and freshly ground black pepper

Break the eggs into a bowl, season with salt and pepper, then add the Parmesan and beat well. Dust the aubergine slices in seasoned flour, dip them into the egg mixture and then coat with the polenta.

Heat the olive oil in a large frying pan and, over a medium-high heat, fry the aubergine slices on both sides until golden brown. Remove, drain on kitchen paper and serve either hot or cold. When eaten hot, they are deliciously crunchy.

# involtini di melanzane alla parmigiana

baked aubergine rolls filled with mozzarella

This is a speciality from southern Italy, where aubergines are found in abundance and are full of flavour. It makes a wonderful vegetarian main course.

I like making the aubergines into *involtini* (rolls), but if you prefer you can make layers of tomato sauce, aubergine slices, Parmesan cheese, mozzarella and basil, which is the traditional way of making this dish. Serve with a green salad for an informal mid-week supper.

**serves 4–6**

1 large aubergine, cut lengthways
   into 6 slices about 5 mm
   (¼ inch) thick

2 tablespoons plain flour

2 eggs, lightly beaten with some
   salt and pepper

olive oil for frying

40 g (1½ oz) Parmesan cheese,
   freshly grated

18 large fresh basil leaves

300 g (11 oz) mozzarella cheese,
   roughly sliced

salt and freshly ground black
   pepper

**for the tomato sauce:**

4 tablespoons extra virgin olive
   oil

1 garlic clove, finely chopped

1 small onion, finely chopped

½ celery stalk, finely chopped

400 g tin of plum tomatoes

To make the tomato sauce, heat the olive oil in a saucepan, add the garlic, onion and celery and sweat until softened. Stir in the tomatoes, season with salt and pepper, then cover the pan and simmer gently for 25 minutes.

Preheat the oven to 200°C (400°F, Gas Mark 6). Dust the aubergine slices in the flour, then dip them in the beaten egg. In a large frying pan, heat some olive oil to a depth of about 1 cm (½ inch), add the aubergine slices and fry on both sides until golden. Remove and drain on kitchen paper. Line the aubergine slices up on a large chopping board, season with salt and pepper, then evenly sprinkle 25 g (1 oz) of the Parmesan over the top. Place 3 basil leaves on each aubergine slice and top with a couple of slices of mozzarella, reserving half the cheese. Then carefully roll each slice up, making sure they are seam-side downwards so they don't open up.

Line a large ovenproof dish (or individual ones) with some of the tomato sauce and place the aubergine rolls on top. Spoon over the remaining tomato sauce and top with the remaining mozzarella slices and Parmesan. Place in the oven and bake for 15 minutes, until the top is very lightly coloured and beginning to bubble.

PaSScOne

# verdure alla griglia

## grilled vegetables

There is nothing more visually appealing than a plate of mixed grilled vegetables. They can be eaten hot or cold, so can be prepared in advance if necessary. If you have a charcoal grill, then you will obviously get a better flavour. Ideal for barbecues for your vegetarian guests!

**serves 4**

1 yellow and 1 red pepper, roasted, skinned and sliced into strips 3–4 cm (1¼–1½ inches) wide (see page 163)

150 ml (¼ pint) olive oil

1 garlic clove, roughly chopped

2 small courgettes

1 aubergine

1 Spanish onion

12 cherry tomatoes on the vine

a few fresh mint leaves, roughly chopped

a few fresh basil leaves, roughly chopped

balsamic vinegar for drizzling (optional)

salt and freshly ground black pepper

Place the roasted pepper slices on a plate and drizzle over a couple of tablespoons of the olive oil. Add the garlic and some salt and pepper and leave to marinate for 15 minutes.

Meanwhile, cut the courgettes and aubergine lengthways into slices about 5 mm (¼ inch) thick. Score each slice in a criss-cross fashion with a small, sharp knife. Peel the onion and cut it into 4 fairly thick slices. Put the vegetables on a lightly oiled ridged grill pan or under a hot grill for a couple of minutes on each side, until just tender. Grill the whole tomatoes, too, until soft.

Arrange the vegetable slices and tomatoes on a serving dish, drizzle the remaining olive oil over them and season with salt and pepper. Sprinkle the mint over the courgettes and the basil over the tomatoes. Arrange the marinated peppers on the dish with or without the garlic, as you wish. I prefer it with!

If you like, you can drizzle some balsamic vinegar over the vegetables to give them extra zest.

PASSIONE

# insalata di arancie e finocchio

## orange and fennel salad

This salad is typical of Sicily, where oranges are grown in abundance. It is eaten all over the South as well, and I remember it was one of my father's favourite salads as a pre-lunch snack to refresh himself and stimulate his tastebuds – rather like an aperitif. The combination of sweet oranges, the aniseed flavour of the fennel and the saltiness of the anchovies make this a very tasty salad indeed.

**serves 4**

4 oranges, peeled, all zest and
   pith removed
8 black olives, sliced
1 large fennel bulb, finely sliced
   (reserve the feathery fronds)
8 anchovy fillets
4 tablespoons extra virgin olive
   oil
2 teaspoons red wine vinegar
salt and freshly ground black
   pepper

Take an orange in the palm of your hand and with a small, very sharp knife cut out the segments from between the membranes, discarding the pips and any pith still attached. Repeat with the remaining oranges.

Place the orange segments and sliced olives in a bowl, then add the fennel and anchovies. Season with salt and pepper (be careful with the salt as the anchovies are already quite salty). Mix in the olive oil and vinegar, leave to marinate for a minute or two and then serve. Decorate with the green feathery leaves from the fennel.

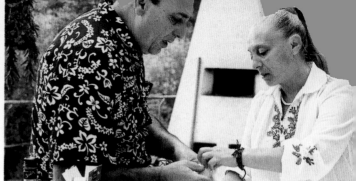

# insalata di carciofi, asparagi e finocchio

salad of raw artichokes, asparagus and fennel

Raw artichokes are surprisingly delicious. They are usually served as a salad with shavings of fresh Parmesan, dressed with extra virgin olive oil and lemon juice. Here I have omitted the Parmesan and added other crunchy, raw vegetables. If you don't like one of the vegetables, you could substitute some raw carrots.

**serves 4**

4 small fresh artichoke hearts, cleaned (see page 162) and very finely chopped

4 small asparagus spears (use just the tips, about 5 cm/ 2 inches), sliced lengthways in half

2 small fennel bulbs, finely chopped

8 chicory leaves, finely sliced in strips

2 small spring onions, finely chopped (optional)

**for the dressing:**

6 tablespoons extra virgin olive oil

4 tablespoons lemon juice

salt and freshly ground black pepper

When you have chopped all the vegetables, set them aside and make the dressing. Place all the dressing ingredients in a large bowl and mix well. Add the chopped vegetables and toss together. Serve immediately with some bread. Makes a lovely, healthy starter!

*Sharing cooking tips with my younger sister Adriana*

# insalata di zucchine con menta fresca

courgette salad with fresh mint

Courgettes are delicious eaten raw, as long as they are firm and fresh and you slice them very thinly. This quantity serves two people as a starter or four as a side dish. The longer you leave it to marinate before serving, the better this salad becomes.

**serves 2–4**

120 ml (4 fl oz) extra virgin olive oil

4 tablespoons balsamic vinegar

1 garlic clove, finely chopped

a handful of fresh mint, finely chopped

4 small courgettes

salt and freshly ground black pepper

Whisk the olive oil and vinegar together with the garlic, mint and some salt and pepper. Trim the ends of the courgettes and, with a potato peeler, slice them lengthways. They have to be wafer-thin. Add the slices to the dressing, mix well and leave to marinate for 10 minutes or more before serving.

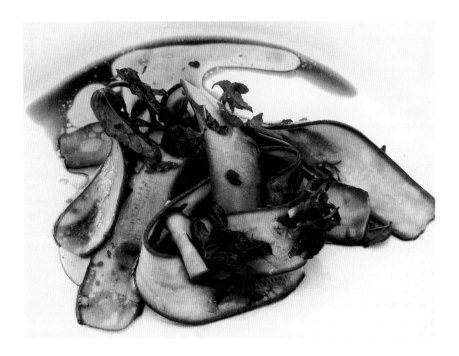

# bietole rosse marinate

marinated beetroot

Fresh beetroot doesn't feature much on Italian menus but I remember it was one of my mother's favourite vegetables, and she would often preserve it. If you follow this recipe, the beetroot will keep for about two weeks in the oil; if you want it to last longer you will have to store it in sterilised jars. Once all the beetroot has been consumed, keep the oil and use it to flavour salads or pasta or to marinate some more beetroot. You need such a lot of olive oil for this recipe that it's a shame to throw it away.

Serve the marinated beetroot as you would pickles – perhaps as an antipasto with some salami or air-dried tuna (*mosciame*).

**serves 6**

650 g (1½ lb) raw beetroot

500 ml (17 fl oz) white or red wine vinegar

2 litres (3½ pints) water

a pinch of salt

**for the marinade:**

2 garlic cloves, sliced

1 tablespoon dried oregano

1 red chilli, finely chopped

500 ml (17 fl oz) olive oil

Wash and scrub the beetroot under cold running water. Place them in a saucepan with the vinegar, water and salt and bring to the boil. Reduce the heat, cover the pan and simmer for about 1¼ hours, until the beetroot are tender. Meanwhile, combine all the marinade ingredients in a bowl and set aside.

Once the beetroot are cooked, drain, place on a cloth and pat dry. Remove the skins with the help of the cloth. Cut into slices, place in the marinade and mix well. Leave for a day before serving. The beetroot will keep for several days in a covered container in the fridge but should be brought to room temperature before serving.

PASSIONE

PASSIONE

# verdure miste sott'olio

## mixed preserved vegetables

Preserving vegetables was very common when I was a child. It was a means of enjoying certain vegetables all year round. Nowadays we can get all sorts of vegetables at any time of year but I still like to preserve them when they are in season. Not only is it an enjoyable task but preserving gives them a different flavour. Here I have chosen peppers and aubergines, which I have preserved raw so they remain nice and crunchy. Serve with a few slices of Parma ham and salami, plus lots of good bread for a delicious antipasto.

**serves 8-10**

600 g (1 lb 5 oz) red and yellow peppers

600 g (1 lb 5 oz) aubergines

150 g (5 oz) salt

800 ml (1⅓ pints) white wine vinegar

3 garlic cloves, thinly sliced length-ways

1 red chilli, thinly sliced

1 tablespoon dried oregano

250 ml (8 fl oz) olive oil

Cut the peppers in half and remove all the seeds and white membrane. Slice lengthways into very fine strips. Peel the aubergines, slice them lengthways and then cut finely lengthways into strips approximately the same size as the peppers.

Keep the vegetables separate. Take 2 plastic containers, one for the peppers and one for the aubergines. Line one container with the peppers, sprinkle with a good handful of the salt, then carry on with layers of peppers and salt, ending up with salt. Place a weight over the top and set aside. Take the other container and do the same with the aubergines. Leave the vegetables for 1½ hours, after which time they will have exuded a lot of liquid.

Take the vegetables in your hands and squeeze out the excess liquid. Place in separate containers, cover each with the vinegar and leave for 1½ hours again.

Drain the vegetables, squeezing out the excess liquid with your hands, and place together in a bowl with the garlic, chilli and oregano. Add the olive oil and mix well. Place in a jar, securing tightly with a lid, and leave for a couple of days before using.

# consigli di gennaro sulla preparazione delle verdure

## Gennaro's vegetable cooking tips

### Artichokes

To prepare artichokes, remove the bottom outer leaves with a small, sharp knife and cut off the stalk. With your fingers, gently open up the artichoke until you can see the hairy choke. Remove it with a small scoop or teaspoon and discard. If you want to use just the hearts, then remove all the leaves except for a few tender inner ones. If your hands get black while cleaning the artichokes, wash them with lemon juice – you will see how quickly the dark stains disappear. Rub the artichokes with lemon juice, too, to prevent discoloration and, if you are not cooking them immediately, keep them in a bowl of water acidulated with lemon juice.

You can cook artichokes in many ways, and even eat them raw when they are young and tender. Simply chop them finely, drizzle with some extra virgin olive oil and lemon juice, then season with salt and pepper. Place on a bed of rocket and top with Parmesan shavings.

### Celery

To obtain maximum flavour, bash celery stalks with the flat of a knife blade before chopping them. Use the leaves as well. Added at the end of cooking, they give a wonderful fresh flavour to the dish.

### Courgettes

Unless you are using very small, fresh courgettes, the white middle part does not really have much flavour. If you have ever eaten plain boiled courgettes you will know what I mean. To make the most of courgettes, cut off the skin in long strips a good 5 mm (1/4 in thick) and discard the white middle part (you could save it to add to vegetable stocks). Slice or chop the green strips according to your recipe.

### Garlic

Before chopping garlic cloves, squash them whole with the skin on for the best flavour.

### Mushrooms

Do not wash mushrooms, whether wild or cultivated. Use a soft brush or slightly damp cloth to clean them. Mushrooms are already full of water and immersing them in more will only destroy their flavour.

## Onions

Soak whole onions in cold water for 30 minutes before peeling. You will find the skin comes off more easily and they will be less pungent when you chop them (so you will be less likely to cry!).

## Parsley

Use the stalks, finely chopped, for stocks and soups. They are very flavoursome.

## Peppers

To roast peppers, place them under a hot grill, turning several times, until the skin goes black. Remove and leave to cool. Peel off the skin, slice the peppers in half and remove the white interior and all the seeds. Then slice according to your recipe.

   For a delicious salad, slice roasted peppers into strips, sprinkle with some extra virgin olive oil, chopped garlic, salt and pepper and leave to marinate for about 15 minutes. This makes a good antipasto with lots of bread. Alternatively, to make a sauce for pasta, place the skinned, deseeded roasted peppers in a food processor or blender and whiz with enough extra virgin olive oil to give a smooth sauce. Season, heat through gently and mix with some cooked penne or tagliatelle.

## Potatoes

If you plan to mash your potatoes, don't peel them. Just wash them to get rid of any dirt, then boil them whole. Once tender, drain and remove the skin, which will peel off very easily. You will find that potatoes cooked this way make much better mash, as they are not so watery.

## Salads

There are now so many different types of salad dressings from cuisines all over the world. There are balsamic dressings, ones made with fancy vinegars, ones flavoured with mustards, spices and herbs – all of these can be delicious, but for me the simple, classic Italian way to dress salads is the best. Place your salad leaves in a large bowl, then sprinkle them quite abundantly with salt and drizzle with two parts extra virgin olive oil to one part white or red wine vinegar. Mix well, using your hands – you will find that this way the dressing coats each leaf.

## Tomatoes

To skin tomatoes, cut a tiny cross in the base of each one with a sharp knife. Place them in a bowl of boiling water for no more than 30 seconds, then drain and place in cold water. Peel off the skins.

# pomodori tomatoes

The tomato played a very important role in our culinary life when I was growing up. It is integral to Italian cooking, the basis for so many sauces, and a delight to eat raw in salads.

I remember the anticipation I felt in late summer when I knew my favourite tomato, the San Marzano, was nearly ripe and ready to eat. This long plum tomato grows close to my home, in the Pompeii valley under the shadow of Mount Vesuvius. The fertile volcanic soil helps to produce what I think is the best-tasting tomato in Italy. These tomatoes were perfect in salads and delicious on their own, drizzled with olive oil and sprinkled with salt.

Because tomatoes were so important to our cuisine, we preserved them for use all year round. These days you can buy tinned tomatoes everywhere, in every corner shop and supermarket, whole or chopped, plain or flavoured with herbs. Tomato purée is readily available in tubes and jars, and sun-dried tomatoes can be bought at most supermarkets and delicatessens. But when I was a child, we had to prepare the tomatoes ourselves. The hard work made us appreciate food much more and brought the family together.

In my house, the preservation of tomatoes was a great ceremony. It was also enormous fun. It was usually in September, when the San Marzano tomato was still available, that the family gathered together and the grand procedure began.

*Papá with my younger sister Adriana on the cellar steps*

We preserved our tomatoes not in tin cans but in small beer bottles made of thick, brown glass. The glass had to be thick to survive the pasteurisation process. A long wooden table was set out in the garden with lots of chairs arranged round it for all the family to sit at. On the table was a vast supply of freshly cleaned beer bottles, a bucketful of corks, fresh basil leaves and kilo upon kilo of washed tomatoes. The tomatoes were cut lengthways into quarters and pushed into the beer bottles along with the odd basil leaf until they were almost full. The bottles were then corked, using a strange gadget. The scene was like a production line, but unlike a factory everyone was cheerful and relaxed, laughing and chatting as they worked.

At the other side of the garden was a large oil drum placed over a tripod. On the bottom of the drum was a raffia sack, folded in two. We placed the filled beer bottles in the drum one by one. Once it was full, water was poured in and another raffia sack placed on top to act as a lid. Then a fire was lit underneath. We took it in turns to sit with the fire all night and make sure it didn't go out until the early hours of the morning, when the process was finished. Once the water had cooled, we removed the beer bottles, dried them and placed them in our store cupboards, ready for use in winter.

We always made huge quantities, enough to ensure a year-round supply for us, as well as our family living in the city who could not make their own. The preservation process was perfect. Even when we found a bottle that was a couple of years old at the back of the cupboard, the tomatoes still tasted good.

PASSIONE

*A local farmer's supply of preserved tomatoes in the kitchen of his home*

These tomatoes didn't taste like the tinned ones you find in the shops; they were something else. There are still families in southern Italy who preserve their tomatoes in this way each year. If I had the time now, I think I would, too.

Besides preserving whole tomatoes, we used to make tomato concentrate to use throughout the winter months in heavy-based sauces for pasta or

meat dishes. The tomatoes were washed and put through a special mincer to extract the pulp. Then the pulp was placed in large, flat, terracotta dishes, covered with nets to keep the flies off and placed on the veranda under the hot August sun for the excess moisture to evaporate.

One member of the family was put in charge of this process. Their duty was to stir the pulp every couple of hours with a large wooden spoon and occasionally sprinkle a few drops of olive oil over the top to prevent a crust forming. The dishes were taken in at night and put out again first thing in the morning. After three or four days, the fresh pulp turned into a thick, delicious concentrate of pure tomato. It was transferred to terracotta jars, drizzled with oil and sealed with greaseproof paper and string.

*Papá on his linen stall with brothers and friends*

# salsa di pomodoro

## basic tomato sauce

This is the most basic Italian tomato sauce and the most widely used with pasta and other dishes. It's always handy to make a large batch and keep in the fridge – although don't leave it for more than about three days. After this time, it is better to make a fresh batch.

**makes enough for 4 servings of pasta**

4 tablespoons olive oil

2 garlic cloves, finely chopped

2 x 400 g tins of plum tomatoes, chopped

a handful of fresh basil, finely chopped

salt and freshly ground black pepper

Heat the olive oil in a large frying pan, add the garlic and sweat until softened. Then add the tomatoes and basil, season with salt and pepper and simmer gently for 25 minutes.

# salsa alla crudaiola

fresh tomato sauce

This is a delicious way to flavour summer pasta dishes or to top bruschetta (see page 194) and crostini (see page 196). Alternatively you could simply serve it as a salad to accompany fish dishes. Make sure you use ripe cherry tomatoes, good-quality extra virgin olive oil and lots of fresh basil.

**makes enough for 4 servings of pasta**

400 g (14 oz) cherry tomatoes,
    cut into quarters

2 garlic cloves, finely chopped

a handful of fresh basil leaves,
    roughly torn

6 tablespoons extra virgin olive oil

salt and freshly ground black pepper

Mix all the ingredients together in a bowl. Leave to marinate for at least 30 minutes. If you don't like garlic, or find 2 cloves too strong, use less or omit it altogether.

If you serve the sauce with pasta you can use it as it is or gently heat it through.

# pomodori in bottiglie

'fresh' tinned tomato sauce

I call this 'fresh' as although I use tinned tomatoes they are not cooked for very long and are only chopped in half, so when served they look and taste quite fresh. They taste just like the tomatoes we used to preserve in beer bottles.

**makes enough for 4 servings of pasta**

2 x 400 g tins of plum tomatoes,
    chopped in half

12 fresh basil leaves

6 tablespoons olive oil

3 garlic cloves, cut into thick slices

salt and freshly ground black pepper

Place the tomatoes and their juice in a bowl with half the basil, add some salt and pepper and mix well. Heat the olive oil in a large pan and add the garlic. When the garlic begins to change colour, remove the pan from the heat and add the tomato mixture. Replace on the heat and cook gently for 4 minutes, until the mixture is bubbling. Stir in the remaining basil leaves.

passione

# ragu di pomodoro

heavy-based tomato sauce

This tomato sauce is used to flavour heavy, meat-based pasta dishes such as the traditional Il Ragu (see page 106-7). You can use it simply as it is if you prefer a heavier tomato sauce. An hour's cooking time should suffice, but if you are cooking pieces of meat in the sauce you will need about two hours. Remember, the longer you cook this sauce, the richer it will become.

**makes enough for 4 servings of pasta**

6 tablespoons olive oil

1 onion, very finely chopped

1 celery stalk, very finely chopped

1 garlic clove, finely chopped

2 x 400 g tins of chopped
   tomatoes

2 tablespoons tomato concentrate or tomato purée, diluted
   in 400 ml (14 fl oz) lukewarm
   water

100 ml (3½ fl oz) red wine

a handful of fresh basil leaves,
   torn

salt and freshly ground black pepper

Heat the olive oil in a large pan, add the onion, celery and garlic and sweat until soft. Add the tomatoes, diluted tomato concentrate or purée and wine. Season with salt and pepper, add the basil and stir well. Bring to the boil, then cover the pan — but not completely, so some of the steam can escape — and reduce the heat. Simmer for about 1 hour, until the sauce is thick and silky. Stir from time to time, checking that there is enough moisture; if necessary add a little more wine or some water.

*Ragu di Pomodoro. Salsa alla Crudaiola and Pomodori in Bottiglie (see pages 170-1)*

PaSSioNE

# insalata di pomodori di camona

green and red tomato salad

Camona, on the lovely, sun-drenched island of Sardinia, is home to the wonderful green tomatoes of the same name. A very good greengrocer may stock them. If not, use plum tomatoes that are not too ripe and try getting some green (i.e. unripe) tomatoes as well. Not only do they add colour but I find them very tasty in a salad.

Tomatoes go well with either fresh basil or dried oregano, but never the two herbs together. If you use oregano, add a few thin slices of sweet red onion to the salad – delicious. Otherwise, keep it simple with fresh basil and the tomatoes.

**serves 4**

2 large red tomatoes, sliced

2 large green tomatoes, preferably Camona tomatoes, sliced

1 garlic clove, finely sliced (optional)

a few fresh basil leaves or 1 teaspoon dried oregano

extra virgin olive oil

salt

Arrange the sliced tomatoes on a plate, scatter over the garlic, if using, followed by either basil or oregano. Sprinkle with salt and drizzle with abundant extra virgin olive oil.

# pomodori al forno

## stuffed tomatoes

Try to buy vine-ripened tomatoes for this recipe, as they tend to have more flavour and are easier to stuff. The only problem is getting them to stand up during cooking; the best thing to do is use a small ovenproof dish and pack them in tightly to keep them upright. Serve warm with a green salad for a light lunch or starter, or even as a side dish to accompany meat or fish.

**serves 4**

**8 medium-sized vine-ripened tomatoes**

**extra virgin olive oil for drizzling**

**8 teaspoons breadcrumbs**

**for the stuffing:**

**6 anchovy fillets, finely chopped**

**a handful of fresh flat-leaf parsley leaves, finely chopped**

**100 g (4 oz) provolone cheese, finely diced**

**6 large green olives, pitted and finely chopped**

**3 tablespoons breadcrumbs**

**1 tablespoon extra virgin olive oil**

Preheat the oven to 200°C (400°F, Gas Mark 6). Slice the top off each tomato, leaving the stalks on so the tops resemble little hats. Set aside. Loosen the tomato seeds and pulp from the flesh with a sharp knife, ensuring that you don't cut into the flesh or pierce the skin. With a teaspoon or small melon baller, remove all the seeds and juice, then leave the tomatoes upside down on a plate for at least 5 minutes to drain.

Meanwhile, place all the stuffing ingredients in a small bowl and mix together well. Fill the tomatoes with the mixture and place them in a small ovenproof dish, tightly packed together so they don't fall over. Drizzle with a little extra virgin olive oil and sprinkle 1 teaspoon of breadcrumbs over the top of each tomato. Bake for 30 minutes, then remove from the oven and place the 'little hats' back on. Leave to stand for a couple of minutes before serving, as the filling is very hot, then drizzle with some more extra virgin olive oil and serve.

funghi mushrooms

I love the changing seasons. It is one of the reasons I live in England. My favourite season has always been the autumn. As September arrives, the summer ends. In Minori, that means the tourists leave, the sea becomes rough and populated with different kinds of fish, the weather changes and there is no more stifling heat. That was always my signal to leave the sea and move to the mountains, where I would lose myself in the forest, picking chestnuts, walnuts and mushrooms.

The first rain brought life to the changing land. The soil developed a rich, musky smell. Out of the blue, the fruits of the earth appeared. Thousands of mushrooms. There is nothing more magical than a glorious, sunny autumnal morning spent roaming the woods in search of these elusive fungi.

I was introduced to wild herbs and mushrooms at an early age. My mother used to take me with her on her collecting trips in the hills and fields. She showed me what was good to eat, what to try and what to leave well alone. She collected herbs and mushrooms for her herbal remedies, but we usually came back with such an abundance of produce that she would also use them for cooking.

I was still fairly young when she sent me out on my own to collect mushrooms and herbs for her. Even then, mushrooms intrigued me. I loved trying to

*Papá with his favourite horse, Cicco*

distinguish the poisonous ones from the edible ones. It was like a game. I sampled them while I was out and about. Then I thought I was immortal; now I know I was just lucky.

I would take the mushrooms back to my mother. She threw away the ones she thought were poisonous and kept the ones she knew were good. I know so much more about mushrooms now and it breaks my heart to think of the priceless specimens she threw away.

I couldn't believe the abundance of wild herbs and mushrooms in the fields and forests when I came to England. It was here that my passion grew, and I was determined to become more knowledgeable. I discovered the delights of truffles in England, not Italy – although I am certain they existed in the forests of my childhood, I just wasn't aware of them.

I still go on regular herb and mushroom collecting forays. Some days I come back with seven or eight different edible species of mushroom – pretty ones, ugly ones, colourful ones, big ones, small ones – they are all delicious. On spring days, I like to go out and search for rocket, wild garlic, dandelions, wild fennel and sorrel.

I love the fact that you can find wild food anywhere – in fields, in parks, by the sea, even on the edge of motorways and in city centres.

**Remember that although many mushrooms are safe to eat, others are highly poisonous and can be fatal. If you pick your own mushrooms, ensure you can identify them with absolute certainty, or go out with an expert.**

PASSIONE

# funghi al funghetto

mushrooms in tomato sauce

This is a traditional way of cooking vegetables in southern Italy. You make a tomato sauce, then add blanched vegetables and continue to cook until the sauce thickens.

**serves 4**

4 tablespoons olive oil

2 garlic cloves, finely chopped

½ small red chilli, finely chopped

400 g tin of plum tomatoes, chopped

a handful of fresh flat-leaf parsley, finely chopped

150 g (5 oz) button mushrooms

150 g (5 oz) baby chestnut mushrooms

salt and freshly ground black pepper

Heat the olive oil in a large frying pan, add the garlic and chilli and sweat until softened. Then add the tomatoes and parsley, season with salt and pepper and simmer gently for 20 minutes.

Meanwhile, bring a saucepan of water to boil, add the mushrooms and simmer for 3 minutes. Drain well, add to the tomato sauce and simmer for about 5 minutes, until the sauce reduces a little. Serve immediately, as a starter with bread, as a side dish or as a main dish, accompanied by a green salad.

# pasticcio di funghi

timbale of mushrooms

This dish is prepared in a very similar way to lasagne but without the pasta. It takes a little organisation, but makes a substantial and delicious vegetarian main course. If you are lucky enough to find large porcini mushrooms, even better.

Instead of the usual tomato sauce, I have made a drier sauce using mushrooms and cherry tomatoes, as the cheese sauce is already runny. If you prefer, you can make it with Salsa di Pomodoro (see page 169).

*The beautiful town of Atrani – the village next to Minori*

serves 4–6

8 large flat mushrooms

plain flour for dusting

3 eggs, beaten

olive or vegetable oil for
   shallow-frying

**for the tomato and mushroom sauce:**

3 tablespoons olive oil

1 garlic clove, crushed but left
   whole

1 onion, finely chopped

1/2 leek, finely chopped

2 large flat mushrooms, cut into
   thin strips

2 tablespoons water

10 ripe cherry tomatoes, cut into
   quarters

a handful of fresh parsley leaves,
   roughly chopped

needles from 1 sprig of fresh
   rosemary, finely chopped

salt and freshly ground black
   pepper

**for the cheese sauce:**

25 g (1 oz) butter

1 heaped tablespoon plain flour

1 litre (1¾ pints) milk

65 g (2½ oz) Parmesan cheese,
   freshly grated

First make the tomato and mushroom sauce. Heat the olive oil in a large pan, add the garlic and cook gently until it begins to colour. Remove and discard the garlic, then add the onion and leek to the pan and sauté until soft. Add the mushroom strips, sauté for a minute, then add the water, tomatoes, parsley and rosemary. Season with salt and pepper and continue to cook for a couple of minutes. Remove from the heat and set aside.

Then make the cheese sauce. Melt the butter in a saucepan, stir in the flour and mix well to avoid lumps. Add the milk and Parmesan, whisking all the time with a balloon whisk, and simmer gently until the sauce thickens. Remove from the heat and season with salt and pepper.

Cut off and discard the black gills from the mushrooms, then slice each mushroom horizontally into 2 or 3 thick slices. Lightly wet the mushroom slices with a little water, dust them in flour and finally coat them with the beaten egg. In a large pan, heat some oil to a depth of about 1 cm (1/2 inch), add the mushroom slices and fry until golden. Remove from the pan and drain on kitchen paper.

Preheat the oven to 200°C (400°F, Gas Mark 6). Pour a layer of cheese sauce over the bottom of an ovenproof dish, then top with a layer of mushroom slices, slightly overlapping, followed by a thin layer of cheese sauce, then the tomato and mushroom sauce. Continue to do this until you have used up all the ingredients, finishing with a layer of cheese sauce. Cover with aluminium foil and bake for 30 minutes. Remove the foil and bake, uncovered, for 5 minutes or until golden brown. Remove from the oven and serve immediately.

# funghi misti saltati

## sauté of mixed wild mushrooms

This is a simple but truly exquisite recipe, especially after a mushroom hunt when you have lots of different varieties. Nothing is more pleasurable than going into the forest on a clear, crisp, autumnal morning and looking for mushrooms. However, if you are not fortunate enough to go out and pick your own, cultivated ones will suffice if you add dried porcini to give that 'wild' flavour. Simply soak 10 g (¼ oz) dried porcini in 120 ml (4 fl oz) lukewarm water for an hour, then add them, together with their soaking water, instead of the stock.

This dish is delicious as a starter, with lots of bread to mop up the sauce, or as an accompaniment to game or meat dishes.

**serves 4**

400 g (14 oz) mixed wild
   mushrooms, such as porcini,
   chanterelles, hedgehog, wood
   blewits

6 tablespoons olive oil

3 garlic cloves, finely chopped
   lengthways

1 small red chilli, roughly chopped

120 ml (4 fl oz) vegetable stock

2 tablespoons roughly chopped
   fresh flat-leaf parsley

salt

Clean the mushrooms with a cloth and brush – do not wash wild mushrooms, as the flavour disappears. Roughly chop any large mushrooms and leave small ones intact.

Heat the olive oil in a frying pan, add the garlic and chilli and sweat gently until softened – do not burn or allow to brown. Raise the heat a little, add the mushrooms and stir well for about a minute. Then add the stock, keep stirring, and cook for 2 minutes longer, until the liquid has evaporated slightly. Stir in the parsley and salt. Remove from the heat and serve immediately.

# tagliatelle con funghi misti

tagliatelle with mixed mushrooms

If you enjoy making the sauté of wild mushrooms on the opposite page and would like to use the same method for a more substantial dish, this is ideal. Fresh or dried tagliatelle are the perfect match for mixed mushrooms. Remember that you can use cultivated mushrooms, adding soaked dried porcini to give that 'wild' taste.

**serves 4**

400 g (14 oz) mixed wild
   mushrooms, such as porcini,
chanterelles, hedgehog, wood
   blewits
6 tablespoons olive oil
3 garlic cloves, finely chopped
   lengthways
1 small red chilli, roughly chopped
120 ml (4 fl oz) vegetable stock
2 tablespoons roughly chopped
fresh flat-leaf parsley
225 g (8 oz) fresh or dried
   tagliatelle
salt
freshly grated Parmesan cheese,
   to serve (optional)

Follow the recipe for Funghi Misti Saltati (see opposite).

Meanwhile, place a large saucepan of lightly salted water on the heat and bring to the boil. Add the tagliatelle and cook until *al dente* (fresh pasta will take only about 1 minute; check the instructions on the packet for dried). Drain the pasta and add to the mushroom mixture. Mix well and serve immediately, sprinkled with some Parmesan if desired.

# insalata di funghi

mushroom salad

Like Funghi Misti Saltati (see page 182), this is a good recipe to make when you have a nice mix of mushrooms. Even if you don't pick them yourself, you can get a good selection of cultivated ones in shops these days. This salad makes a lovely starter with lots of good bread, or can be made in advance and served at parties.

**serves 4**

300 g (11 oz) mixed wild mushrooms, such as porcini, chanterelles, hedgehog, wood blewits

1 litre (1¾ pints) water

juice of 2 large lemons

6 tablespoons extra virgin olive oil

¼ red chilli, finely chopped

2 garlic cloves, finely chopped

a handful of fresh flat-leaf parsley, finely chopped

10 large black or green olives, sliced

salt

lemon wedges, to serve

Clean the mushrooms with a cloth and brush – do not wash wild mushrooms, as the flavour disappears. Roughly chop any large mushrooms and leave small ones intact.

Put the water, lemon juice and some salt in a saucepan, bring to the boil and add the mushrooms. Simmer for about 4 minutes. Meanwhile, in a bowl, combine the olive oil, chilli, garlic, parsley and olives.

Drain the mushrooms and immediately add them to the olive oil marinade. Mix well, check the seasoning, then leave to cool. Serve with lemon wedges.

# funghi sott'olio

## preserved mushrooms

Because I am only able to get local wild mushrooms in season, I love to preserve them so I can enjoy them later in the year. In Italy it is traditional to pick porcini during late summer and autumn and then preserve them to enjoy at Christmas lunch with the antipasto. If you preserve them in small jars, they make ideal Christmas presents.

**serves 10-12**

2 litres (3½ pints) water

500 ml (17 fl oz) white wine vinegar

1 glass of white wine

20 g (¾ oz) salt

2 bunches of fresh rosemary

3 cloves

2 red onions, cut into quarters

1 red chilli, left whole

1 whole garlic bulb, cut in half

2 kg (4½ lb) mixed mushrooms (either wild or cultivated), cleaned

1 litre (1¾ pints) olive oil

Place the water, vinegar, wine and salt in a large saucepan and bring to the boil. Add the rosemary, cloves, onions, chilli and garlic. Then add the mushrooms, bring back to the boil and simmer for 5 minutes.

Drain the mushrooms and the other ingredients (onions, garlic, rosemary and chilli) and spread them out on clean cloths to dry. When they are cold, pick them up carefully with tongs and place in a sterilised 2 kg (4½ lb) preserving jar (or several smaller jars). Cover with the oil and leave without the lid on for 2 hours. Ensure that the oil has seeped through to the bottom, cover with the lid and store in a cool, dark place for 1 week before eating (it can be left for up to 3 months).

Once opened, keep refrigerated and consume within a couple of weeks.

PASSIONE

# cotolette di funghi puffball

puffball cutlets

Puffballs are strange-looking creatures. They are large, white mushrooms resembling foot-balls and can grow to quite an extraordinary size. They grow wild in fields from the end of August until mid-October and can be found all over the English countryside. If you ever find any, the best way to cook them is to coat them in breadcrumbs and shallow-fry.

They make a hearty English breakfast with scrambled eggs and bacon, or an Italian starter or snack with some preserved vegetables.

**serves 2–4**

1 medium-sized puffball, weighing
   about 150 g (5 oz)
2 eggs, lightly beaten with some
   salt and pepper
100 g (4 oz) fresh breadcrumbs
olive oil for shallow-frying

Clean the puffball by removing any dirt with a small brush or damp cloth. Cut into slices about 1.5 cm (2/3 inch) thick. Dip into the beaten egg, then coat in the breadcrumbs.

Heat some oil in a large frying pan, add the mushroom slices and fry on both sides until golden brown. Remove and drain on kitchen paper. Serve hot or cold.

PASSIONE

# tramezzini snacks

**E**veryone snacks in Italy. Known as *merende* in my day, snacks are part of the fabric of life. Many people only drink a small black coffee before leaving the house in the morning but then stop in a bar on their way to work and buy a croissant or a sandwich. Mid-morning and mid-afternoon, they like to have a little something, quite apart from lunch. There have been *rosticcerie* – shops dedicated to snacks – in Italy for as long as I can remember, and certainly long before fast food became a way of life in Britain and the USA. *Rosticcerie* fall half-way between a restaurant and a coffee bar and sell a whole assortment of delicious nibbles: little pizzas, salami, potato and mozzarella croquettes, endless freshly made sandwiches, hot sausages and roast quail, all ready to eat.

The Italian equivalent of the kebab is a million times more delicious. We love *porchetta*, or spit-roast suckling pig, which is sold from specialist shops and stalls. The succulent slices of pork are served on hunks of rustic bread all over Italy.

All the towns and villages around Minori had a feast day for their patron saint. It was a great excuse to travel all over the region and sample local

*Papá on the right with his friends Costantino and Mino at the local bar*

delicacies. Because there were so many villages scattered over the mountains, there was sure to be a feast day within a few kilometres every weekend during the summer. Local farmers would bring their produce to sell, housewives prepared the village speciality to serve to visitors, and local shops put on their best displays of gastronomic delights. I would meet up with a gang of friends and we would visit as many as we could reach. We called them *merende* days because we set out to try as many different delicacies as we could find.

*Tramonti, a hilltop village on the Amalfi coast*

PASSiONE

# spiedini aromatici di mozzarella e acciughe

mozzarella and anchovy skewers

This is a very tasty snack using stale bread, mozzarella and anchovies. The hot bread will be nice and crisp and the anchovies add a tangy taste, making these snacks ideal to serve with pre-dinner drinks.

Use the cheaper mozzarella, such as *fior di latte*, which is ideal for cooking and melting. There is no point using the more expensive buffalo mozzarella, which should only be eaten fresh.

**makes 4**

12 slices of stale baguette, cut about 1 cm (½ inch) thick

4 slices of mozzarella cheese

50 g (2 oz) butter

5 anchovy fillets, finely chopped

a few fresh chives, finely chopped

freshly ground black pepper

Preheat the oven to 180°C (350°F, Gas Mark 4). Take 4 wooden skewers and thread 3 slices of bread through the crusts on each one, placing a piece of mozzarella on the middle slice. Put the skewers on a baking sheet and place in the oven for about 10 minutes, until the mozzarella has just melted and the bare slices of bread become crisp.

Meanwhile, make the anchovy sauce. Melt the butter in a small pan, add the anchovies and mix well.

Pour a little anchovy sauce over each bare slice of bread. Sprinkle chopped chives over the mozzarella, grind over some black pepper and serve immediately.

# bruschetta

bruschetta

Bruschetta is a classic Italian snack that has become increasingly popular in restaurants and pizzerias in the UK. I suppose it is Italy's answer to garlic bread. It is very simple to make and is an extremely nutritious snack at any time of day.

**1-2 slices of bread per person**

slices of stale, leftover bread
   (ciabatta is good)

a few garlic cloves, peeled

abundant extra virgin olive oil

chopped ripe tomatoes (optional)

fresh basil leaves, roughly torn
   (optional)

salt

Toast the bread on both sides, or grill it on a ridged chargrill pan. Remove and immediately rub the garlic cloves over one side of the bread while it is still warm – you will see the garlic melt into the toast. Sprinkle with salt, drizzle with lots of extra virgin olive oil and top with a few chopped tomatoes and fresh basil, if desired. Serve immediately.

PASSIONE

# crostini

crostini

Crostini are slices of bread (baguette is ideal) that have been grilled or slowly baked in the oven, then topped with almost anything you like. In Italy, people often serve a selection of crostini as a starter or with pre-dinner drinks. Alternatively, they are a handy way of using up stale bread to serve as a snack instead of the usual sandwich.

Good ideas for toppings include olive paste, artichoke paste (both available in good delis), chicken liver pâté (a favourite in Tuscany), a little Salsa alla Crudaiola (see page 170) or a few preserved vegetables (see page 161).

# pasta fritta

pasta snacks

This is my version of crisps! When you make a batch of fresh pasta and have some left over, roll it out, cut it into a taglierini or tagliolini shape (see page 39) and deep-fry. Flavoured with some salt, it makes a fun snack for children or can be served with drinks. You could also flavour it with freshly ground black pepper, a little crushed dried chilli, some dried oregano or anything else you like.

**serves 4-6**

leftover pasta dough
  (see page 29)
olive oil for deep-frying
salt

Roll out the dough with a pasta machine to make very thin sheets. Then cut out the thinnest spaghetti shape you have on your machine. As each batch comes out of the machine, roll it into neat nests.

Heat abundant olive oil in a large saucepan or a deep-fat fryer. Add the pasta nests a few at a time and fry for about 1 minute, until golden brown. Drain on kitchen paper. Sprinkle with some salt and serve warm or cold.

# carpaccio di scamorza

carpaccio of smoked mozzarella cheese

I dedicate this recipe to Kate Adie, journalist and war correspondent. While at passione for dinner one evening, she was talking about the various meals she had eaten around the world and mentioned her favourite Italian dish, which she had had about 20 years ago – a salad of very thinly sliced cheese dressed with raw vegetables and olive oil. She had had this only once, in a restaurant in Bologna, and had never found it on other menus. I quickly went downstairs to the kitchen and recreated the dish. When I took it upstairs, wow, it certainly brought back memories for her!

It's extremely simple to prepare and makes a wonderful light snack or a sophisticated starter. You can get hard-smoked scamorza cheese at most good Italian delis. Just remember you will need a good sharp knife, as everything has to be sliced wafer-thin. If you have a mandolin, use that, or the finest slicer on your food processor.

**serves 4**

2 small scamorza cheeses

½ small shallot, very finely sliced

1 small celery heart, very finely sliced (including the leaves)

4 button mushrooms, very finely sliced

juice of 1 lemon

4 tablespoons extra virgin olive oil

freshly ground black pepper

Remove the hard skin from the cheeses and cut them lengthways into extremely thin slices. Don't worry if you don't get a whole slice, as long as the pieces are wafer-thin. Arrange them evenly on serving plates and top with the shallot, celery and mushrooms. Grind over some black pepper, then drizzle over the lemon juice and olive oil. Leave to marinate for 5–10 minutes and serve with good bread.

# crocchette di fave

stuffed broad bean cakes

Broad beans are good not only eaten whole but also when mashed and made into a dough. This recipe takes a little time to prepare but the result is worth the work. The little cakes are delicious hot or cold, or they can be made in advance and reheated in the oven.

makes 36

300 g (11 oz) fresh or frozen
   broad beans
250 g (9 oz) plain flour
2 eggs
50 g (2 oz) butter, softened
1 teaspoon dried yeast, diluted
   in 1 tablespoon lukewarm water
olive oil for deep-frying
salt and freshly ground black
   pepper

for the filling:
250 g (9 oz) ricotta cheese
1 egg
3 tablespoons freshly grated
   Parmesan cheese
3 tablespoons fresh chives,
   finely chopped
a pinch of nutmeg

Blanch the broad beans in a large pan of boiling water for
1 minute, then drain well and cool in cold water. Peel off the
skins. Place the beans in a food processor and whiz until mushy.
Transfer to a large bowl, add the flour, eggs, butter, yeast mixture and some salt and pepper and mix well with your hands
until you obtain a smooth dough. Cover with a cloth and leave in
a warm place for about 30 minutes, until slightly risen.

Meanwhile, make the filling. Put all the ingredients in a bowl and
mix to a smooth paste. Season with salt and pepper.

Shape the dough into balls the size of golf balls. On a lightly
floured work surface, roll each ball of dough out into an oval
shape about 3 mm ($^1/_8$ inch) thick. Place a tablespoon of the
filling on it and roll it up, pinching the edges together to close.

Heat the olive oil in a large, deep saucepan or a deep-fat fryer.
Deep-fry the croquettes, a few at a time, for 2–3 minutes, until
golden brown. With a sharp knife, cut in half on the diagonal.
Drain on kitchen paper and serve hot or cold.

Not only was I the only boy in the family, I was also extremely skinny when I was young. My mother was determined to build me up, and she went out of her way to bring me *merende* throughout the day. She would embarrass me daily by tracking me down when I was out playing with my friends and calling me over to drink a concoction of freshly beaten eggs and sugar, which she prepared in front of us all. I remember my face burning as I felt my friends watching us.

Another daily ritual was the afternoon snack. But this I shared with my friends. When we met up to play after school, we all carried a paper parcel from our mothers – precious bundles ready for the inevitable moment when all of us were starving. Somehow it was always at five o'clock, and whether we were on the beach, in the mountains, in the village or the fields, all play would stop. Frantic bartering went on until everyone had the snacks they fancied, then there was a moment of silence. We were like an orchestra. Once we started to eat you could hear a symphony of appreciative, 'Mmms.' We even looked like musicians, holding our baguettes carefully as if they were flutes and clarinets.

I learned a great deal about food from these snack sessions, because as soon as we had eaten the first few mouthfuls, stories would begin about where the food came from. 'I killed the pig', or 'My father milled this flour', and 'My mother grew these vegetables', or 'I preserved these fruits'. We educated each other about food. Many of my childhood friends have since become chefs. I realise now that the quality of those simple afternoon snacks was outstanding. We had bread with all sorts of fillings: pork dripping and sea salt, salami, aubergine and tomato, mozzarella and fruit.

*A view of the Mediterranean from a villa in Praiano*

202 PaSSione

# arancini di riso

## deep-fried stuffed rice balls

These typically Sicilian snacks are a great way of using up leftover risotto. Traditionally they are filled with different stuffings, such as minced meat or mixed vegetables, and sold as take-away snacks, but to make them simpler you could omit the filling. I have chosen a simple filling of peas and mozzarella. When deep-fried, the mozzarella melts and tastes wonderful as you bite into the *arancino*. I suggest you make lots, as once you start eating them you can't stop!

**makes 25**

plain flour for dusting

2 eggs, beaten

breadcrumbs for coating

olive oil for deep-frying

**for the risotto:**

1.5 litres (2½ pints) vegetable stock

3 tablespoons olive oil

1 onion, finely chopped

300 g (11 oz) Arborio or other Italian risotto rice

4 tablespoons freshly grated Parmesan cheese

salt and freshly ground black pepper

**for the filling:**

1 tablespoon olive oil

1 tablespoon finely chopped onion

100 g (4 oz) frozen peas

2 tablespoons water

75 g (3 oz) mozzarella cheese, diced

Make the risotto following the basic recipe on page 61, omitting the butter (or use any leftover risotto you have). Spread the risotto evenly over a baking tray and leave to cool.

Meanwhile, make the filling. Heat the olive oil in a small pan, add the onion and sweat until soft. Then add the peas, water and some seasoning. Cover with a lid and cook for a few minutes, until the peas are tender. Leave to cool.

Take a little of the risotto and form it into a ball, roughly the same size as a golf ball. You will find it easier if you wet your hands with cold water. Make an indentation in each ball and place a few peas and a couple of cubes of mozzarella in it. Reshape the ball so the filling is in the centre and completely covered by the risotto. Dust with a little flour, then coat with beaten egg and finally coat in breadcrumbs.

Heat some olive oil in a large, deep saucepan or in a deep-fat fryer. Add the risotto balls a few at a time and fry for 2–3 minutes, until golden brown. Drain on kitchen paper and serve hot or cold.

All my friends had nicknames, and they were all called after a food or snack. Alfonso was named Muscione, which means something soft, because when we raided the fig trees in the afternoons he would clamber to the top and feel the figs until he found a soft one. Then there was Sperlungone, named after a long bread, because his mother never made ordinary bread. Hers was always very long, and his roll used to reach from his mouth to his stomach. There was Muzecatella, which means little bite, named because he always took tiny bites of his snack. Biscotti earned his nickname because he liked his snacks very sweet. A very dear friend of mine is nicknamed Melanzana, which means aubergine. In all the years I knew him, he ate an aubergine sandwich every afternoon. A few years ago, someone sent me a postcard of my village. Melanzana was in the background perched on a wall, eating what I would swear was an aubergine baguette.

Lupino got his name from his love of lupins, a type of bean. To give them their flavour, lupins used to be dried and put into big cloth sacks, which were then suspended by chains from the cliffs and rocks that overhung the sea. Lupino famously jumped off the rocks armed with his penknife, with the idea of helping himself to an illicit serving of beans. He made tiny little holes in the sacks and filled his swimming trunks with the lupins. It was a very dangerous mission. The waves crashed against the rocks and he could easily have drowned.

I can remember eating all day long. We certainly weren't starving. We learned about food by talking to the local bakers, butchers and restaurateurs. We couldn't help but learn about food because the knowledge was all around us.

PASSIONE

# la vera pizza napoletana

genuine Neapolitan pizza

You get so many varieties of pizzas these days that I don't blame the Italians for wanting to make it DOC (quality controlled) like wine. Everyone has their own taste and I respect that, but recently I saw chicken tikka pizza on an Indian take-away menu. I do think that this is going a bit far – let's leave pizza to the Italians and chicken tikka to the Indians!

I once had the opportunity of spending some time at the Pizza Academy in Naples, and it is really strict about how the dough is made and what toppings can be used. This is my recipe for the original Neapolitan pizza, which started off as a means of using up the house-wife's leftovers: bread dough, tomatoes, cheese and whatever else they had in their cupboard – which I am sure was not chicken tikka!

PASSIONE

**makes 2 large pizzas**

**for the dough:**

500 g (1 lb 2 oz) Italian '0' flour
  or strong plain flour

2 teaspoons salt

10 g (1/4 oz) fresh yeast

325 ml (11 fl oz) lukewarm water

a few dried breadcrumbs or some
  semolina for sprinkling

**for the topping:**

300 g (11 oz) tinned plum
  tomatoes, drained

4 tablespoons extra virgin olive
  oil, plus extra for drizzling

25 g (1 oz) Parmesan cheese,
  freshly grated

a few fresh basil leaves, or some
  dried oregano

150 g (5 oz) mozzarella cheese,
  roughly chopped

salt and freshly ground black
  pepper

Put the flour and salt in a large bowl. Dissolve the yeast in the lukewarm water and gradually add to the flour, mixing well until you obtain a dough. If you find the dough too sticky, just add a little more flour. Shape the dough into a ball and leave to rest, covered with a cloth, for 5 minutes. Knead the dough for 8–10 minutes, until smooth and elastic, then split it in half. Knead each piece for a couple of minutes and then shape into a ball. Sprinkle some flour on a clean tea towel and place the dough on it, then cover with a slightly damp cloth. Leave to rise in a warm place for 30 minutes.

Meanwhile, place the tomatoes in a bowl, crush them slightly with a fork, season with salt and pepper and mix well. Preheat the oven to 250°C (500°F, Gas Mark 10) – if your oven doesn't go this high, just heat it to its highest setting and cook the pizzas for a few minutes longer if necessary.

Sprinkle some flour on a clean work surface and with your fingers spread one piece of dough into a circle about 35–40 cm (14–16 inches) in diameter. Make the dough as thin as a pancake but be careful not to tear it, and make the border slightly thicker. Repeat with the other ball of dough, then sprinkle some breadcrumbs or semolina over 2 large, flat baking trays and place the pizza bases on them.

Spread a little of the tomato evenly over each base – not too much, or the pizzas will be soggy. Drizzle with the olive oil, sprinkle over the Parmesan, add a few basil leaves or some oregano and top with pieces of mozzarella. Place in the hot oven for 7 minutes (a couple of minutes longer if you prefer your pizza crisp). Remove from the oven, drizzle with a little more olive oil and eat immediately.

# frittata di cipolle e porri con crosta di parmigiano

leek and onion omelette rolls in a Parmesan crust

This is a fun and unusual omelette recipe. Once the omelette is cooked, you make a cheese crust by lining a good-quality non-stick frying pan with grated Parmesan and letting it cook until it melts into a whole piece but is still pliable. The omelette is placed over it and the whole thing rolled up like a swiss roll.

**makes 10–12 slices**

**2 eggs**

**2 tablespoons olive oil**

**1 small onion, finely sliced**

**1 leek, finely sliced (the white part only)**

**50 g (2 oz) Parmesan cheese, freshly grated**

**salt and freshly ground black pepper**

In a bowl, beat the eggs with a fork and season with salt and pepper. Heat the olive oil in a non-stick 20 cm (8 inch) frying pan, add the onion and leek and sweat until softened. Pour in the beaten eggs, reduce the heat and cook until golden brown underneath. Flip over and cook the other side. Remove from the pan and set aside.

Wipe out the frying pan so it is dry and clean. Place on a very low heat and sprinkle the Parmesan cheese evenly over the base. Cook for 1 minute. You will notice the Parmesan sticking together and forming a crust. Gently, with a spatula, lift out the Parmesan crust and place it on a chopping board or a clean work surface. Immediately place the omelette on top, carefully roll it up with the crust and cut into slices with a sharp knife. It is important to do this quickly or the Parmesan will be too hard to work with.

Either eat straight away or serve cold as part of an antipasto – or take it on a picnic.

PASSiONE

**pane** bread

In Italy bread forms the basis of every meal. In fact, Italians hold bread in such high esteem that when we want to say that someone is a good person we say they are like a piece of bread (*è come un pezzo di pane*).

At home, my father did most of the cooking but my mother baked the bread. She could easily have bought it but she insisted on making her own. I felt she was showing us how much she loved us through her baking. She put her heart and soul into it and filled the bread with her happiness as she prepared it for us to eat.

Mamma used a wood-fired oven. She always baked bread on a Thursday and there was a certain purposeful excitement in the way she lit the oven the night before. She cooked the loaves slowly so they would stay fresh all week. In the morning, she would be up at five to stoke the fire. I would hear the crackling of the burning twigs. The smell would slowly waft through the house and infiltrate my dreams. I would wake up hungry, jump out of bed and run into the smoke-filled kitchen. There I would find three or four beautiful, warm, massive round loaves on the table. The smell was irresistible and it took all my willpower not to grab the bread and tear it apart.

When I make bread now, I put a little bit of my soul into it. Baking bread is the most wonderful part of the working day for me. Early every morning at the restaurant, I spend a couple of hours making the bread for that day. I walk into the cold, empty kitchen before the rest of the world is up. The first thing I do is switch on the oven. Then I take the yeast out of the fridge. To me, it is a living thing to be cared for. It is cold and I can hear it crying out to be fed, so I give it its breakfast. I add the flour, then the water, and watch the big bubbles explode as I mix it together. It gives me such pleasure to watch. Then I leave the dough to rise.

Once it has risen, I take some of the dough and ask it what shape it would like to be today. I tease it into long rolls, round rolls, *filone*, *filoncino*, large *campagnia* loaves – so many gorgeous, voluptuous shapes. The focaccia and filled rolls are made last. I always find something delicious to top my focaccia. Sun-dried tomatoes, olives, onions and rosemary are favourites. For my rolls I choose the freshest seasonal fillings – such as grilled vegetables, wild garlic, pesto – or mixed cheese and salami.

While the bread is in the oven, I leave the kitchen and go out on to the street for some fresh air. The moment I go back downstairs is magical. The smell of bread baking never fails to overwhelm me with sweet, nostalgic memories of my childhood.

It may sound crazy but if I bake in the afternoon the bread is never as good. Maybe it is because the ingredients are living things. I think the dough knows from the way I handle it if I'm miserable. In the afternoons I am too tired to put the amount of love into the mixing that I do in the mornings. If I'm happy and energetic, the bread always tastes much better.

The Greek word for bread translates literally as everything. I couldn't agree more. I believe bread gives you everything you need.

passione

# impasto di pane

## basic bread dough

I make most of my dough-based recipes from this basic dough. Bread may seem complicated and an effort to make, but I suggest you try it – there is no more appealing cooking smell than that of your own bread, and certainly no other bread can match the taste. You will find that this bread keeps for days without going mouldy. After a day or so it might go hard, but place it in a hot oven for a few minutes and it will taste freshly made again.

**makes 1 loaf, 1 small focaccia or 10 rolls**

800 g (1¾ lb) Italian 'O' flour
   or strong plain flour

200 g (7 oz) semolina

20 g (¾ oz) salt

25 g (1 oz) fresh yeast

700 ml (24 fl oz) lukewarm
   water

semolina, coarse polenta or
   dried breadcrumbs for
   sprinkling

In a large bowl, mix the flour, semolina and salt together. Dissolve the yeast in the lukewarm water and pour into the flour. Mix well until you obtain a soft but not sticky dough. Turn out on to a lightly floured work surface and knead well for about 5 minutes, until smooth and elastic. Place the dough on a clean tea towel, brush the top with some water to prevent it drying out, then cover with another clean tea towel. Leave to rise in a warm place for about 30 minutes or until doubled in size. Knock the risen dough back down and shape it into 2 round loaves. Place on a baking sheet sprinkled with semolina or breadcrumbs, cover with a tea towel and leave in a warm place again until doubled in size. Preheat the oven to 240°C (475°F, Gas Mark 9).

Place the loaves on the bottom shelf of the oven and bake for 25 minutes. The way to test if a loaf is ready is to bang it gently on the bottom: if it sounds hollow, it is ready. Remove from the oven and leave to cool. This bread is delicious eaten on the day it is baked. It will keep for about a week and is great sliced and used for bruschetta (see page 194), crostini (see page 196), toast or breadcrumbs (see below).

**Breadcrumbs**   Place some sliced stale bread on a baking tray and bake in the oven at 120°C (250°F, Gas Mark ½) for about an hour to dry out completely. Remove from the oven and whiz in a food processor. Store in an airtight container.

# grissini

breadsticks

Grissini originally come from Turin and the name is associated with the long, thin, industrially produced ones wrapped in cellophane, which are widely available and found in many Italian restaurants. Home-made grissini are completely different – they are thicker, fresher and much tastier. Serve with other breads at the table at mealtimes, or as a snack with a slice of Parma ham wrapped round each one.

**makes 12**

300 g (11 oz) Italian '0' flour or
   strong plain flour
200 g (9 oz) semolina, plus extra
   for sprinkling
2 teaspoons salt
1 tablespoon olive oil
15 g (½ oz) fresh yeast
350 ml (12 fl oz) lukewarm water

Make the dough in the same way as the Basic Bread Dough (see page 215), adding the olive oil just before you pour in the yeast liquid. Leave to rise until not quite doubled in size. Then, on a lightly floured work surface, gently roll out the dough into a rough square, about the thickness of your finger. Lightly brush with a little water and sprinkle over a handful of semolina. With a pastry wheel or sharp knife, cut out strips approximately 2 cm (¾ inch) wide. Don't worry about the length; they can be different sizes.

Sprinkle some semolina on a baking tray. Place the grissini on the tray about 2 cm (¾ inch) apart, gently pulling them out a little at either end as you do so. If you want the grissini to have a rounded shape, roll each strip gently with your fingers before placing it on the baking tray.

Leave in a warm place for 30 minutes or until doubled in size. Meanwhile, preheat the oven to 240°C (475°F, Gas Mark 9).

Place the grissini in the oven and bake for 10 minutes. Remove from the oven and turn the temperature down to 110°C (225°F, Gas Mark ¼). When the oven has cooled down to this temperature, put the grissini back in for 35 minutes or until golden brown. Remove from the oven and leave to cool.

PASSIONE

As a child, I was like one of the Bisto kids when bread was being made. The smell was so enticing. There is nothing like it.

I loved having bread in the morning. My mother often made me something called a *scodella* from any leftovers. This delicious treat was simply a bowl of bread with milk, sugar and cinnamon. It was like nectar to a hungry boy.

Every day, we children were packed off with a generous wedge of bread. We would all meet up and search the orchards for ripe fruit to eat with it. My favourite was figs. When they were ready, I found fig trees, climbed to the top with my loaf and gorged on the ripe fruit. The problem with having a passion for figs was that I was nearly always caught out. The trees gave off milk, which made me sticky and scratchy. It was very difficult to remove – even though I jumped straight into the sea afterwards to try to wash it off.

When the bread was fresh and warm, my little friends and I headed for the village *pasticceria* to have scoops of chocolate ice cream put into the middle. The result was an inspiration. The memory of the ice cream melting into the warm dough still makes my mouth water.

I was always threatened with a prison diet of bread and water when I mis-behaved as a child. It was never much of a deterrent, though, because I loved bread so much that I actually looked forward to the punishment!

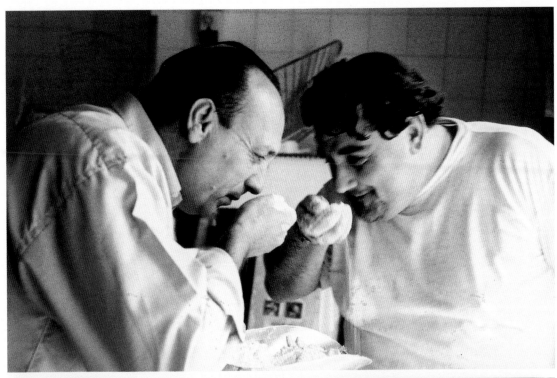

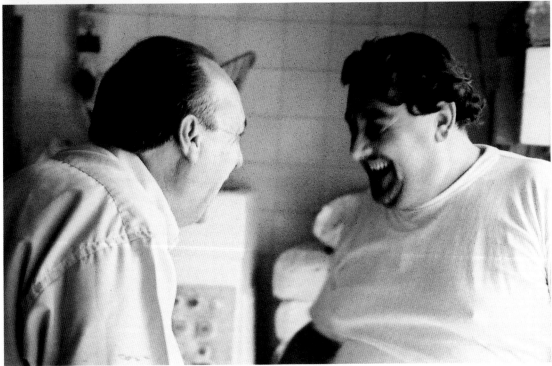

*With Giuseppe Apicella the local baker in Tramonti*

# pane rustico

bread with salami, cheese and eggs

This has to be one of my favourite types of bread. It was traditionally made by farmers' wives as a filling lunch for their husbands while working in the fields, using up all their left-overs of ham, salami, cheese and even pork fat (scratchings). I make this bread at Easter time, as the eggs, which are placed around the ring, make it look very pretty and seasonal for Easter Sunday breakfast.

   Make sure the eggs are at room temperature, as if they are cold they interfere with the rising of the dough. Securing them with strips of dough prevents them exploding in the oven. The eggs come out perfectly cooked and make a delicious addition to this substantial loaf.

100 g (4 oz) salami, cut into
   small cubes

100 g (4 oz) pancetta, cut into
   small cubes

100 g (4 oz) prosciutto, cut into
   small cubes

100 g (4 oz) provolone cheese,
   cut into small cubes

100 g (4 oz) pecorino cheese, cut
   into small cubes

100 g (4 oz) Parmesan cheese,
   freshly grated

2 tablespoons coarsely ground
   black pepper

600 g (1 lb 5 oz) Italian '00' flour
   or strong plain flour

1 teaspoon salt

25 g (1 oz) fresh yeast

450 ml ( ¾ pint) lukewarm water

semolina or dried breadcrumbs for
   sprinkling

6 eggs

Place all the meat and cheese in a bowl with the black pepper, mix well and set aside.

Mix the flour and salt together in a large bowl. Dissolve the yeast in the lukewarm water and add to the flour. Mix with your hands, gradually incorporating all the flour, until you obtain a soft, slightly sticky dough. Turn out on to a floured work surface and knead for about 3 minutes or until smooth, adding more flour to the work surface if necessary. Break off a piece of dough about the size of a tennis ball and set aside. Spread the remaining dough out into a rough circle and add the meat and cheese mixture, kneading it into the dough until evenly combined. Continue to knead for a couple of minutes, then roll the dough into a large sausage shape about 65 cm (26 in) long and seal the ends to form a ring.

Sprinkle some semolina or breadcrumbs on a large, flat baking tray and place the ring on it. Make 6 deep incisions around the top of the ring with a sharp knife and with your fingers enlarge each one to make a pocket. Place an egg lying flat in each pocket.

Take the reserved piece of dough, roll it out into a rough square and cut out 12 strips approximately 7.5 cm (3 inches) long. Place 2 strips criss-cross over each egg, brushing them with a little water so they stick well. Cover the loaf with a cloth and leave in a warm place until doubled in size. Meanwhile, preheat the oven to 220°C (425°F, Gas Mark 7).

Bake the loaf for 30 minutes or until golden. Delicious served hot or cold.

# focaccia con aglio e rosmarino

focaccia with garlic and rosemary

I remember having focaccia as a child, although we did not know it by that name. We would flatten leftover bread dough and drizzle it with extra virgin olive oil and sea salt. This would often be my breakfast. When I became a chef, I discovered that this simple bread was commonly known as focaccia, and during my many travels over Italy I saw it being made in different ways with various toppings and even stuffed. I used to bring these ideas back to England with me and develop them further.

You can top focaccia with almost anything you like – cherry tomatoes, olives, grilled vegetables, herbs, but always with extra virgin olive oil and sea salt. In this basic recipe, I have given you just a few simple ingredients – garlic, rosemary, oil and sea salt – which together make a delicious topping. Focaccia is best served warm straight from the oven but if you make it in advance you can always reheat it in a hot oven for a few minutes just before serving. It makes an ideal accompaniment to meals instead of bread rolls,and can even be sliced in half and filled with some ham and cheese to make a substantial sandwich.

*Minori with the Mediterranean in the distance*

PASSIONE

**for the dough:**

300 g (11 oz) Italian '0' flour or
    strong plain flour

200 g (7 oz) semolina, plus extra
    for sprinkling

2 teaspoons salt

15 g (½ oz) fresh yeast

350 ml (12 fl oz) lukewarm water

**for the topping:**

2 tablespoons extra virgin olive
    oil, plus extra for drizzling

2 large garlic cloves, finely
    chopped

needles from 3 fresh rosemary
    branches, finely chopped

1 teaspoon flaky sea salt,
    preferably Maldon

freshly ground black pepper

Preheat the oven to 240°C (475°F, Gas Mark 9). Make the dough in the same way as the Basic Bread Dough (see page 215). You will need a baking tray about 37.5 x 27.5 cm (15 x 11 inches). After the first rising, place the dough on a lightly floured work surface and roll out into a rectangular shape roughly the size of the baking tray. Warm the baking tray in the hot oven for about 10 seconds, then remove and sprinkle with semolina. Place the rolled-out dough on the tray and pour the extra virgin olive oil in the middle. With your fingers, spread the oil all over the dough. Leave for 5 minutes, then poke the dough all over with your fingers to make indentations. Sprinkle the garlic and rosemary on top, followed by the sea salt and some black pepper. Leave to rest in a warm place for 30 minutes (a good place is on the hob, if it is directly above the oven).

Bake for about 15 minutes, until evenly golden brown. Check the focaccia from time to time, as domestic ovens often colour one side and not the other, so turn the baking tray round accordingly. Once cooked, remove from the oven and immediately drizzle some olive oil all over. Leave to cool, then cut into squares.

This bread is delicious eaten on the day it is baked, but it will keep for a few days and you can freshen it up in the oven for a few minutes just before serving.

# panini con verdure alla griglia e parmigiano

mixed grilled vegetable and Parmesan rolls

This is an excellent way of using up leftovers. I have suggested grilled vegetables here, but you can also use ham, salami, cheese, even pesto (see page 50). The rolls look good and are very tasty – great for taking on picnics or adding to your bread basket.

**makes about 18**

**for the dough:**

300 g (11 oz) Italian 'O' flour or
    strong plain flour

200 g (7 oz) semolina, plus extra
    for sprinkling

2 teaspoons salt

15 g (½ oz) fresh yeast

350 ml (12 fl oz) lukewarm water

extra virgin olive oil for drizzling

**for the filling:**

2 tablespoons olive oil

3 tablespoons freshly grated
    Parmesan cheese (or Cheddar,
    if you prefer)

1 large courgette, cut into strips
    and grilled

1 aubergine, cut into strips and
    grilled

1 yellow and 1 red pepper,
    roasted and cut into strips
    (see page 163)

a handful of cherry tomatoes
    (optional)

salt and freshly ground black
    pepper

Make the dough in the same way as the Basic Bread Dough (see page 215). After the first rising, place it on a lightly floured work surface and roll out into a rectangle about 3 mm (⅛ inch) thick. Drizzle with the olive oil and sprinkle the cheese all over. Cover with the grilled vegetables and season with salt and pepper. Gently roll up lengthways like a swiss roll, tucking in any filling that escapes at either end.

With a sharp knife, slice into rolls about 3 cm (1¼ inches) wide. Sprinkle some semolina on a baking tray and place the rolls on it. Place a cherry tomato on a few of the rolls, if desired. Leave to rest for 20 minutes. Meanwhile, preheat the oven to 240°C (475°F, Gas Mark 9). Bake the rolls on the top shelf of the oven for 12 minutes or until golden brown. Remove from the oven and immediately drizzle with extra virgin olive oil.

*My schoolfriends who I used to share my merende with: Gennaro, Alfonso, Franco, Geraldo and the taller boy at the back is Pepino*

# schiacciata della vendemmia

sweet tart with harvest grapes

At harvest time in Italy it is traditional to put aside some grapes to consume over Christmas. They become deliciously sweet and squashy and make a perfect filling for a pie. I am not suggesting you preserve grapes for this recipe, as nowadays you find them all year round. Use the sweet varieties, such as Muscatel. Don't be alarmed by the large quantity of cinnamon – the taste is not at all overpowering.

**serves 4–6**

20 g (¼ oz) fresh yeast

165 ml (5½ fl oz) lukewarm
  water

300 g (11 oz) Italian '00' flour

1 teaspoon salt

dried breadcrumbs, coarse
  polenta or semolina for
  sprinkling

450 g (1 lb) white or black
  grapes

5 tablespoons extra virgin olive
  oil

65 g (2½ oz) caster sugar

1 tablespoon ground cinnamon

1 branch of fresh rosemary, plus
  a few sprigs to decorate

icing sugar for dusting

Dissolve the yeast in the lukewarm water and set aside. Sift the flour into a large bowl, mix in the salt and make a well in the centre. Gradually pour in the yeast mixture, mixing it with the flour to make a soft but not sticky dough. Turn out and knead on a lightly floured surface for about 10 minutes, until smooth and elastic. Divide the dough into 2 balls, cover with a tea towel and leave to rest for 5 minutes.

Preheat the oven to 200°C (400°F, Gas Mark 6). Roll out one of the balls of dough into a round about 2 mm (¹/₁₂ inch) thick and 15 cm (6 inches) in diameter. Sprinkle a large baking tray with breadcrumbs or semolina then lift the dough on to it. Set aside a small bunch of 8–10 grapes and arrange the rest over the dough, leaving a border of about 2.5 cm (1 inch) all around. Drizzle with 3 tablespoons of the olive oil, sprinkle over 50 g (2 oz) of the sugar and all the cinnamon. Then sprinkle over the rosemary needles.

Roll out the other half of dough to the same size and place this over the filling, pressing down the edges well. Trim away any excess and crimp the edges with your fingers so that the pie is well sealed. Drizzle the remaining olive oil over the top and sprinkle with the remaining sugar. Place in the oven and bake for 10 minutes, then place the reserved grapes on top with a few sprigs of rosemary. Bake for a further 10 minutes until pale gold and lightly caramelised. Dust with icing sugar and serve warm.

PASSIONE

**dolci** desserts

have a very sweet tooth and adore puddings and cakes. When I make them, I use traditional methods to try to recapture the tastes of my childhood. I like to create rustic puddings flavoured with sweet spices such as cinnamon.

It would be no exaggeration to say that I have spent my whole life working with food. I earned my very first wages at the local *pasticceria*, which was owned by the father of a good friend of mine. He was exactly as you would imagine the owner of a cake shop to be, with a chubby, smiling face and a big belly from eating too many of his own cakes. When I went round to my friend's house, I was always given a job to do. Usually it was skinning almonds. Not the nicest job in the world but it paid good money – enough to fund my trips to the cinema.

The almonds were gathered from just outside Minori. Sacks full of them were brought down from the mountains and put outside in the sun to dry. The nuts were cracked and shelled, then given to me to peel – one by one. I was equipped with two buckets of water, one hot and one cold. I had to soak the almonds in the hot water, take them out, peel them and then drop them into the cold. I ate as many as I provided for the shop but a blind eye was turned.

It was a wonderful cake shop. When I passed it in the morning, the smell of baking was good enough to stop you in your tracks. Italy still has good *pasticcerie* but the local, seasonal element has disappeared. My friend's father

*Posing as a cowboy aged 9*

used fresh eggs, freshly milled flour from the village mill and fruit from local orchards. He baked for the shop every day: all kinds of pastries, local speciality biscuits, sponge cakes, jam tarts, chocolate cake and ice cream. Everyone in the village loved him, and he was often requested to make special cakes for weddings, parties and feasts. People would come in with their own recipes or bring in their own spices to be added to their cakes. He would nod and smile and agree to their wishes, but I knew that he never really stuck to the recipes he was given, and generally added a few spices of his own. He always produced a masterpiece and the ladies of the village adored him for it.

I was very lucky in my choice of friends. One of them, Antonio, had a father who owned a coffee shop in the village. It sold all sorts of things besides coffee, and the house speciality was a beautiful lemon sorbet. He made it from a huge block of ice, plus sugar, lemon juice and zest – nothing else. A big aluminium spoon slowly turned on the ice, mixing in the other ingredients until it was smooth and sweet like a cream. You could smell the lemons from 200 metres away.

It was Antonio's job to zest the lemons and he was always made to do this before he could come and play with me. If I was in need of a playmate, I helped him out. We would sit together grating the lemons for the zest and then squeezing out the juice. Of course, I did have an ulterior motive: his father would give us a big portion of sorbet with honey on top when we were done. I learned to make sorbet from this man. Not long ago, I returned to Italy and went to see him. He is very old now but he remembered me. 'Gennarino,' he said (which is what he called me all those years ago; it means little Gennaro), 'do you remember the lemons?'

PASSIONE

PaSSiONE

# torta di limone

## lemon tart

This lemon tart is not made in the traditional way with sweet shortcrust pastry; instead the filling is poured into a puff pastry case. If you enjoy making puff pastry, then do make your own, but it is such a lengthy procedure that I find the ready-made version is fine – especially if you use fresh rather than frozen. I have added ricotta to the filling, which makes it lovely and creamy. Also there is no cooking involved in making the filling, so you don't run the risk of ruining it, which can happen with a lemon curd type of filling.

**serves 10**

100 ml (3½ fl oz) water

1 tablespoon caster sugar

zest of 2 lemons, cut into julienne
  (thin strips)

250 g (9 oz) puff pastry

**for the filling:**

4 eggs, separated

250 g (9 oz) caster sugar

juice of 3 lemons

25 g (1 oz) butter, melted

250 g (9 oz) ricotta cheese,
  sieved

25 g (1 oz) plain flour

First you must remove the bitterness from the strips of lemon zest. To do this, place the water and sugar in a small pan over a moderate heat and stir until the sugar has dissolved. Stir in the lemon strips, raise the heat and bring to the boil. Reduce the heat and simmer for a couple of minutes. Drain, discard the liquid and dry the lemon strips on a kitchen cloth. Leave to cool.

Grease a 25 cm (10 inch) loose-bottomed tart tin with a little butter, then dust it lightly with flour. Roll out the puff pastry thinly on a lightly floured work surface. Use to line the tin, making sure it comes slightly above the edge. Place in the fridge until you are ready to use.

Preheat the oven to 180°C (350°F, Gas Mark 4). To make the filling, beat the egg yolks and sugar together with an electric beater until light and fluffy and doubled in volume. Add the lemon juice and butter and mix well. Stir in the sieved ricotta, sift the plain flour over the top and whisk well to remove any lumps.

In another bowl, whisk the egg whites until they form stiff peaks. Fold them into the lemon mixture, pour into the pastry case and arrange the lemon strips evenly on top. Bake for 40 minutes, until just set. Leave to cool, then gently remove the tart from the tin and transfer to a plate.

# frutta cotta

dried fruit compote with rum

You can buy a wonderful array of dried fruit in supermarkets and healthfood shops and liven it up with spices and rum. This is so simple to prepare that it is worth making a large batch and storing it in sterilised airtight jars. It will keep for a couple of months. Serve with some mascarpone or whipped cream for a delicious, warming winter dessert.

**serves 6–8**

grated zest and juice of 1 lemon

grated zest and juice of 1 orange

2 sprigs of fresh rosemary

1 cinnamon stick

6 cloves

½ teaspoon fennel seeds

½ teaspoon black peppercorns

500 g (1 lb 2 oz) caster sugar

500 ml (17 fl oz) water

1 kg (2¼ lb) mixed dried fruit, such as prunes, apricots, figs, raisins, apples, pears and peaches

200 ml (7 fl oz) dark rum

Put the lemon and orange zest and juice, rosemary, cinnamon, cloves, fennel seeds, peppercorns, sugar and water in a large saucepan and bring to the boil, stirring occasionally to dissolve the sugar. Reduce the heat, cover the pan and simmer gently for 5 minutes. Add the hardest fruit, such as prunes, first and simmer for 3 minutes, then add the rest of the fruit and simmer for 5 minutes.

Remove from the heat and add the rum. Stir well and leave to stand, covered, for at least a day before use. Heat through gently before serving.

PASSIONE

# fragole fresche con salsa di fragole

fresh strawberries with strawberry sauce

**For a simple summer dessert with minimum effort but maximum taste, this is ideal. If you like, you can serve it with good-quality vanilla ice cream.**

**serves 4**

450 g (1 lb) strawberries, cut into
    quarters

sprigs of fresh mint and icing
    sugar, to decorate (optional)

**for the sauce:**

20 g (¾ oz) butter

75 g (3 oz) caster sugar

¼ lemon

200 g (7 oz) strawberries, cut in
    half

First make the sauce. Put the butter and sugar in a saucepan and place over a gentle heat. Spear the lemon quarter with a fork and use it to stir the butter and sugar until the butter has melted and the sugar has dissolved. Press the lemon with the fork to squeeze out all the juice, then discard it. Stir in the halved strawberries, then remove from the heat and push the mixture through a sieve. Leave to cool.

Pour the sauce on 4 serving plates, then top with the fresh strawberries. Decorate with sprigs of mint and sprinkle with icing sugar, if desired.

# gelato passione

limoncello and strawberry ice cream

This recipe was devised by my friend Albino Barberis who makes the best ice cream this side of Milan. He came up with the idea when we opened passione, combining limoncello liqueur, which comes from the Amalfi coast, with wild strawberries because of my fascination for wild food. The result was outstanding and it has become a firm favourite on our dessert menu. I make it with cultivated strawberries but if you want to treat yourself to wild strawberries, then even better!

serves 6-8

225 g (8 oz) strawberries

3 egg yolks

65 g (2½ oz) caster sugar

300 ml (½ pint) double cream

150 ml (¼ pint) full-fat milk

250 ml (8 fl oz) limoncello liqueur

grated zest of ½ lemon

Put a large plastic container in the freezer ready for the ice cream. Slice half the strawberries quite thinly and set aside. Push the remaining strawberries through a fine sieve, retaining only the pulp and discarding the pips. Set aside.

Beat together the egg yolks and sugar. Put the cream and milk in a saucepan and bring gently to the boil. As it begins to boil, remove from the heat and beat in the egg mixture. Return to a low heat and cook for about 1 minute, stirring all the time with a wooden spoon, until slightly thickened. Remove from the heat and fold in the sliced and sieved strawberries. Then stir in the limoncello and lemon zest. Remove the container from the freezer and pour in the mixture until it is about three-quarters full (if you have extra mixture, pour it into another plastic container). Leave to cool, then place, uncovered, in the freezer.

After half an hour, remove and stir well, then replace in the freezer. Leave for another half an hour and repeat the procedure a few times until the ice cream is frozen. Alternatively, if you have an ice-cream machine, churn the ice cream until it thickens, then place in a container in the freezer.

You can serve this anyway you like – here it's in my Mamma's favourite glasses.

# panna cotta con menta fresca

fresh mint panna cotta drizzled with honey

Panna cotta literally translated means 'cooked cream' and that's basically what it is. You can try all sorts of different flavourings – this one is especially light and subtle with the cool, fresh mint. It's a very simple dessert to make, and it should be prepared in advance to give it time to set. I find it sets best if you make it the night before. It will keep for 3–4 days in the fridge.

**serves 4**

3 gelatine leaves

250 ml (8 fl oz) double cream

250 ml (8 fl oz) milk

25 g (1 oz) caster sugar

10 fresh mint leaves, finely
   chopped

a couple of drops of vanilla
   extract

4 tablespoons runny honey

a few chocolate shavings
   (optional)

Place the gelatine leaves in a bowl of cold water and leave to soften for about 5 minutes. Put the cream, milk, sugar, mint and vanilla in a small saucepan and bring gently to the boil. As soon as it begins to bubble, remove from the heat, cover with a lid and leave to rest for 5 minutes. This is done to allow the mint to infuse. Strain the cream through a fine sieve and discard the mint.

Drain the gelatine leaves and squeeze out any excess water with your hands. Add the soaked gelatine to the cream mixture and stir well, making sure that the gelatine melts. The mixture will take on an oily appearance – don't worry, this is because of the gelatine and is quite normal. Pour the mixture into 4 ramekins or dariole moulds and place immediately in the fridge. Leave for at least 4 hours, until set.

To serve, run a knife round the edge of each panna cotta and then turn the mould upside down on to an individual serving dish to tip it out. Drizzle some runny honey on top and scatter with a few chocolate shavings, if desired. If using ramekins, you don't have to tip the panna cotta out if you don't want to; just drizzle the honey on top and serve in the ramekins.

PASSione

# semifreddo di mandorle e cioccolato bianco

semifreddo of almonds and white chocolate

Semifreddo is a classic Italian dessert, which is served straight from the freezer but does not set as firm as ice cream. It is ideal for the warmer months and can be made in advance and kept in the freezer until you need it. I have used individual dariole moulds here but you could use one large mould, such as a loaf tin, and serve it sliced.

serves 6

3 egg yolks

75 g (3 oz) caster sugar

75 g (3 oz) white chocolate, finely chopped

275 ml (9 fl oz) whipping cream

for the *croccante* (praline):

25 g (1 oz) caster sugar

100 g (4 oz) blanched almonds, roughly chopped

3 tablespoons water

First make the *croccante*. Place the sugar in a small, heavy-based pan over a moderate heat and stir with a wooden spoon until it begins to caramelise and turn golden brown. At this stage, add the almonds and water and mix well together. Remove from the heat, pour the mixture on to a lightly oiled baking tray or marble board and leave to cool.

Whisk the egg yolks and sugar together in a bowl until light and fluffy and increased in volume. Break up the cooled *croccante* quite roughly and add it to the egg mixture, together with the white chocolate. In a separate bowl, whip the cream to stiff peaks, then fold it into the mixture. Line six 9 cm (3½ inch) dariole moulds with clingfilm, fill them with the mixture and place in the freezer for at least 2 hours, until frozen. To serve, remove from the freezer and leave at room temperature for a few minutes, then turn out on to plates and peel off the clingfilm.

# pastiera di grano

Neapolitan Easter wheat and ricotta tart

This dessert is believed to date back to pagan times, when Neapolitans would offer all the fruits of their land to the mermaid, Partenope, in spring: eggs for fertility, wheat from the land, ricotta from the shepherds, the aroma of orange flowers, vanilla to symbolise faraway countries and sugar in honour of the sweet mermaid. It is said that the mermaid would take all these ingredients, immerse herself in the sea of the Bay of Naples and give back to the Neapolitans a dessert that symbolised fertility and rebirth. The recipe as we know it today came from Neapolitan convents, and nuns would make it for rich nobles of the area.

My mother and aunts would always make it at Easter. It is still made today, at home as well as in pastry shops throughout the Campania region. In Naples, Easter wouldn't be Easter without a Pastiera di Grano. Wheat sounds like a strange ingredient for a tart but it really is delicious, especially with the delicate flavour of orange-flower water. Pre-cooked wheat is sold in tins in Italian delis, and orange-flower water can be found in supermarkets.

serves 12

400 g tin of pre-cooked wheat

120 ml (4 fl oz) milk

½ teaspoon vanilla extract

250 g (9 oz) ricotta cheese

5 egg yolks

200 g (7 oz) icing sugar, plus
    extra for dusting

120 g (4½ oz) mixed candied
    peel, finely chopped

1½ tablespoons orange-flower
    water

grated zest of ½ orange

2 egg whites

First make the pastry. Sift the flour on to a work surface and make a well in the centre. Add the eggs, sugar, butter and half the lemon zest (reserve the rest for the filling) and lightly blend everything together with your fingertips until you have a smooth dough. Wrap in clingfilm, chill for 1 hour, then roll out thinly and use to line a 25 cm (10 inch) loose-bottomed tart tin. Place in the fridge until ready to use. Do not discard the pastry trimmings; shape them into a ball, wrap in clingfilm and place in the fridge.

Preheat the oven to 170°C (325°F, Gas Mark 3). Place the wheat, milk, 1 tablespoon of the remaining lemon zest and the vanilla extract in a small saucepan, mix well and bring to the boil. Reduce the heat and simmer gently until the wheat has absorbed all the liquid. Remove from the heat and leave to cool.

Mash the ricotta with a fork and beat in the egg yolks until light and fluffy. Sift in the icing sugar and beat until well incorporated, then beat in the candied peel, orange-flower water, the remaining

**for the sweet shortcrust pastry:**
400 g (14 oz) Italian '00' flour
3 eggs
100 g (4 oz) caster sugar
150 g (5 oz) butter, at room
  temperature, diced
grated zest of 1 lemon

lemon zest and the orange zest. Stir in the cooled wheat mixture. In a separate bowl, whisk the egg whites until stiff. Then fold them carefully but thoroughly into the ricotta and wheat mixture.

Remove the pastry case from the fridge and pour in the mixture. Roll out the remaining pastry quite thinly and cut it into 2.5 cm (1 inch) strips roughly the length of the cake tin. Arrange the strips criss-cross over the tart roughly 2.5 cm (1 inch) apart, trimming off any excess and pressing the ends against the edge of the pastry case to seal. Place in the oven and bake for 50 minutes, until lightly browned but still moist. Leave to cool, then sift over some icing sugar to decorate.

*A Madonna on the wall of a farmer's kitchen in the hills above Minori*

# torta al cioccolato e vino rosso

chocolate and red wine cake

Chocolate and red wine go well together, so what better way to combine them than in a cake? This cake is light, moist and simple to prepare. For a special occasion, coat with chocolate sauce (see page 244) and decorate with chocolate curls and a sprig of flowering rosemary.

**makes a 20 cm (8 inch) cake**

200 g (7 oz) butter, softened

250 g (9 oz) caster sugar

4 eggs, beaten

25 g (1 oz) cocoa powder

250 g (9 oz) plain flour

1 teaspoon baking powder

½ teaspoon ground cinnamon
  (optional)

100 ml (3½ fl oz) red wine

½ teaspoon vanilla extract

150 g (5 oz) plain chocolate
  drops

Preheat the oven to 180°C (350°F, Gas Mark 4) and lightly grease a loose-bottomed 20 cm (8 inch) cake tin.

Cream the butter and sugar together until light and fluffy. Gradually beat in the eggs. Then sift in the cocoa powder, flour, baking powder and cinnamon, if using, and fold in. Mix in the red wine and vanilla extract, then fold in the chocolate drops.

Pour the mixture into the cake tin and bake for 1 hour, until a skewer inserted in the centre comes out clean. Remove from the oven and allow to cool in the tin, then turn out. Coat with chocolate sauce (see page 244) and chocolate curls, if desired.

PASSIONE

*My sister Adriana eating chocolate cake with Manuela and Rubin*

# salsa al cioccolato

## chocolate topping

This lovely, rich chocolate sauce is ideal for covering cakes, as when cool it sets and goes quite hard. It can also be used to pour over ice cream or panna cotta (see page 238). In both cases, use immediately after making, before it gets the chance to set. If necessary, make a large batch and keep it for up to a week in the fridge; just place whatever quantity you need in a bowl set over a pan of hot water to melt before using.

**makes enough to cover two cakes**

120 ml (4 fl oz) single cream

150 g (5 oz) plain chocolate, broken up

1½ teaspoons cocoa powder

1½ teaspoons glucose syrup

25 g (1 oz) butter

1 tablespoon sugar

Place all the ingredients in a bowl set over a pan of hot water and stir constantly until the chocolate has melted and the sauce has a smooth, silky consistency. Pour through a sieve, if necessary, to strain out any lumps of cocoa powder. Leave to cool slightly (only a minute or two) before covering the cake.

*Gennaro and Fortunata's eldest daughter Michela*

# torta alle pere

pear cake

This cake is deliciously moist and can be served either as a dessert or at teatime. Use William pears for best results. The glaze is simple to make but you could always do without it – it doesn't really affect the taste of the cake but just gives it a nice, shiny glow!

**makes a 25 cm (10 inch) cake**

2 eggs

1 egg yolk

150 g (5 oz) caster sugar

50 g (2 oz) butter, cut into small
  chunks

1 tablespoon runny honey

3 tablespoons full-fat milk

150 g (5 oz) plain flour

1 teaspoon baking powder

a pinch of salt

1 teaspoon vanilla extract

5 pears

4 tablespoons apricot jam, to
  glaze (optional)

Preheat the oven to 180°C (350°F, Gas Mark 4). Lightly grease a 25 cm (10 inch) round shallow cake tin with butter and line the base with a circle of greaseproof paper.

In a bowl, beat the eggs, egg yolk, sugar, butter and honey together until light and fluffy. You will find this easier and quicker with an electric beater. Gradually add the milk, beating well. Then sift the flour, baking powder and salt over the top and fold in with a metal spoon, adding the vanilla extract too. Core and dice 3 of the pears and mix them in.

Pour the mixture into the prepared cake tin. Core and thinly slice the 2 remaining pears and arrange them on top. Bake for 45 minutes, until the cake is risen and golden brown. Remove from the oven and leave to cool in the tin, then turn out. If you want to glaze the cake, make up the apricot glaze by diluting the apricot jam with a little water and then heating it gently, stirring until smooth. Sieve the warm glaze and brush it immediately over the top of the cake.

A tiny old lady, round as a barrel, ran the smallest, most magical shop in Minori. With a stern expression, she presided over a fabulous array of sweets, chocolates and small pastries, but there was a kindly twinkle in her small, dark eyes.

Her shop was scarcely bigger than a telephone box, yet it was packed with an amazing variety of tantalising delicacies. Everything was handmade. We children thought she was magic, and believed our parents when they told us that a fairy worked with her, sprinkling fairy dust over her sweets.

Pastries were filled with pâtisserie cream made from eggs that had been laid that morning, and flavoured with chocolate. There were tarts filled with ricotta and cherries, apples and cream, and all kinds of fruit. There was nougat, too, made with sugar, almonds and honey. The little *signora* stood with her arms folded across her chest, the trays of sweets before her covered in white muslin cloths. It was pure theatre. She waited until we were breathless with anticipation before lifting the muslin very slowly to reveal the mouth-watering displays and release the most tantalising smells.

I was lucky. I had the chance to taste her sweets now and then because my grandfather would send me on errands to her shop and always gave me a little extra money for myself. The fairy lady always chanted: 'What do you want? How much have you got? Has your Granddad sent you?' When I close my eyes, I can still hear her. She would wrap my grandfather's order in beautiful crisp, coloured paper. And then she would make a smaller parcel for me. She seemed to read my mind, and always put in the very sweets I had been fantasising about. Needless to say, my parcel was opened and devoured almost as soon as I left the shop.

*This is like the tree I used to rest under to watch the sea and collect pine kernels*

# biscotti rococo

## spicy almond biscuits

This is an old recipe from Naples. The exotic spices reflect the type of ingredients introduced to ancient Naples by the Arabic invasions. In fact, these biscuits taste more like a North African speciality than an Italian one. Stored in an airtight container, they will keep for about two weeks. They are delicious served at teatime, or after dinner as an alternative to the classic Tuscan cantuccini, for dipping into a dessert wine such as Passito di Pantelleria or Vin Santo.

**makes about 40**

300 g (11 oz) plain flour

200 g (7 oz) ground almonds

1 sachet of Easyblend yeast

25 g (1 oz) butter, diced

2 tablespoons finely grated lemon zest

2 tablespoons finely grated orange zest

150 ml (¼ pint) sweet white wine

1 egg, beaten, plus beaten egg, for brushing

150 g (5 oz) mixed candied peel, finely chopped

150 g (5 oz) whole almonds, roughly chopped

1 teaspoon ground cinnamon

a pinch of nutmeg

icing sugar, for dusting

Preheat the oven to 180°C (350°F, Gas Mark 4). Mix the flour, ground almonds and yeast together in a large bowl. Add the butter and rub it in with your fingertips until the mixture resembles breadcrumbs. Add the lemon and orange zest, the wine, egg, candied peel, almonds, cinnamon and nutmeg and mix well, preferably with your hands, to form a soft dough. Form into golf ball shapes, then on a lightly floured surface roll into sausage shapes about 12.5–15 cm (5–6 inches) long. Shape each one into a ring, overlapping the ends slightly and pressing them together to seal (like mini bagels).

Place on baking trays lined with greaseproof paper and brush with beaten egg. Bake for 20–25 minutes, until golden brown. Dust with icing sugar and serve.

PASSIONE

# formaggi

## an Italian cheese selection

Cheese can be served before or instead of dessert, and although more popular eaten this way in northern Italy it is now also becoming the trend in the South. Traditionally in the South, cheese is consumed as part of the antipasto course.

I love the cheese course, which is often the highlight of a meal. There are so many varieties and you can combine them with different accompaniments to make it a real talking point. When buying cheese, look out for fully ripened, good-quality specimens, even if you have to travel a little to buy the best. I always bring back some cheese from Italy, as several excellent local types are not available in the UK. Nevertheless, you can get many good varieties in Italian delis and specialist cheese shops nowadays.

Here are some tips on serving cheese as part of an Italian meal.

Take the cheese out of the fridge and leave it at room temperature for about 4 hours before serving. This softens it and its flavour becomes more pronounced.

If serving cheese as part of an antipasto, use a fresh one such as buffalo mozzarella, drizzled with lots of extra virgin olive oil, scamorza or caprino (Italian goat's cheese).

To make up a selection, choose a couple of hard cheeses, such as Parmesan and pecorino, a semi-soft cheese such as Taleggio or provolone, and two soft cheeses – one blue-veined, such as gorgonzola or dolcelatte, and one plain, such as caprino. Four or five cheeses are sufficient; too many and the tastebuds get confused. Serve with some taralli (a southern Italian, crisp, twice-baked savoury biscuit), fresh bread or plain biscuits and some fresh fruit or celery. Always accompany with a good red wine or a full-bodied white.

If you serve just one cheese after dinner, it should be something quite special, such as Castelmagno or Formaggio di fossa served with my special chilli relish (see opposite). Alternatively, a good-quality gorgonzola or dolcelatte drizzled with honey and served with a few walnuts is a great way to end a meal.

Good accompaniments to cheese include pears, grapes, walnuts and fresh broad beans.

Mostarda di Cremona is also excellent with cheese. This is a preserve made of candied fruits and mustard and is available in mild and hot versions. It can be bought in jars from good Italian delicatessens.

*The cheeses overleaf are (clockwise from top left): buffalo mozzarella, ricotta, provolone, Taleggio, pecorino and Parmesan*

# salsina piccante con pere

pear and chilli relish

This wonderfully tangy relish makes a perfect accompaniment to very mature hard cheese such as pecorino, or a selection of after-dinner cheeses. It also goes well with cold meats. Apart from grilling the pears, there is no cooking involved. Stored in attractive jars, the relish makes an ideal present, together with a hunk of good-quality hard cheese.

**makes about 1 kg (2¼ lb)**

3 pears, weighing about 350 g (12 oz)

icing sugar for dusting

4 large, fresh medium-hot red chillies, roughly chopped

500 g (1 lb 2 oz) mostarda di Cremona (preferably the hot variety), any pips removed

375 g (13 oz) marmalade, preferably thick-cut

Cut the pears in half and core them. Cut in half again and then again. Cut into 2 mm (1/12 inch) dice. Arrange on a large, flat baking tray and dust all over with icing sugar. Place under a hot grill for about 10 minutes, until the pears have caramelised.

Meanwhile, place the chillies, mostarda di Cremona and marmalade in a food processor and whiz until smooth (if you are using fine-cut marmalade, don't add it to the food processor). Transfer to a large bowl (fine-cut marmalade should be mixed in now). Add the caramelised pears and mix well.

Fill one large or several small storage jars with the mixture. It will keep for a couple of months.

# indice

## index

Note: page numbers in italics refer to illustrations.

# ringraziamenti

## acknowledgements

Sarah Warmsley for patiently listening to all my stories and putting them to paper so beautifully. Liz Przybylski for spending many hours in the kitchen with me taking down the recipes and then writing them up. Gennaro D'Urso for his support and encouragement throughout and all his helpful suggestions. Heather Holden-Brown for her enthusiasm throughout the project and for being such fun in Italy! Vanessa Courtier for her excellent taste in props and for styling the book so beautifully. Jason Lowe for being the quickest photogra-

pher I have ever come across. Angela Boggiano for her calm and patience in recreating my recipes during the photoshoot. Jane Middleton for being so thorough in checking and rechecking all the text. Jo Roberts-Miller for all her hard work and efficiency in putting the book together. Georgina, Eleanor and all the team at Headline for their support. Pietro Pesce for his helpful hints. Enzo Zaccarini for the best fruit and veg in London. Steve and Janice Lanning for the great idea. Mutti Spa who have helped my passion for food by supplying such beautiful tomatoes. Rossella and Franco Roi for their superb olive oil. Louise Holland for all her help. All my kitchen crew at **passione** – Mario, Roberto, Margherita, Massimo, Mustapha and Thomas for being so marvellous in holding the fort during the time off I had to take to write this book. Luigi Bonomi, my agent, for making this happen! And last but not least, Jamie Oliver, who once used to learn from me and now I learn from him.

**People in Italy during the photoshoot** Fortunata D'Urso for organising our trip. Peppe D'Urso for arranging transport and for finding that lovely goose! Adriana Contaldo, my baby sister, for her props and help during our stay. Angela Fusco and Luca del Gaizo of the Salumeria Angela in Vettica for their help with the shopping. Giuliano and Peppino Ruocco of the antique shop in Minori for supplying props. Antonio Ruocco, the pasta-maker from Minori, for supplying us with his wonderful pasta. Salvatore de Riso of Pasticceria de Riso in Minori for his wonderful cakes and ice-cream. Preziosa D'Amato for showing us her pasta-making skills. Agostino Amato – Antica Latteria di Tramonti – for showing us round his cheese factory. Signor Basilio – farmer – for showing us his gorgeous pigs and rabbits. Valentino Esposito for his wonderful limoncello.

*With Liz and Gennaro outside* **passione**